MINDFULNESS-BASED ART THERAPY ACTIVITIES

Mindfulness-Based Art Therapy Activities

CREATIVE TECHNIQUES TO STAY PRESENT, MANAGE DIFFICULT FEELINGS, AND FIND BALANCE

Jennie Powe Runde, MFT, REAT

ROCKRIDGE
PRESS

As of press time, the URLs in this book link or refer to existing websites on the internet. Rockridge Press is not responsible for the outdated, inaccurate, or incomplete content available on these sites.

First Rockridge Press trade paperback edition 2023

Rockridge Press and the Rockridge Press logo are trademarks or registered trademarks of Callisto Media Inc. and/or its affiliates in the United States and other countries and may not be used without written permission.

For general information on our other products and services, please contact our Customer Care Department within the United States at (866) 744-2665, or outside the United States at (510) 253-0500.

Paperback ISBN: 979-8-88650-122-3 | eBook ISBN: 979-8-88650-248-0

Manufactured in the United States of America

Interior and Cover Designer: Heather Krakora
Art Producer: Melissa Malinowsky
Editor: Alexis Sattler
Production Editor: Rachel Taenzler
Production Manager: Riley Hoffman

Cover and interior illustrations © Anna Gudimova/iStock/Getty Images
Author photo courtesy © Sarah Deragon

10 9 8 7 6 5 4 3 2 1 0

To Chris,
who always sees
the best in me.

CONTENTS

INTRODUCTION

If you're feeling overwhelmed and burned out, you're not alone. Going through a stressful time can be difficult, but it can also be an opportunity to gain insight, develop self-compassion, and find new tools to cultivate balance and calm.

As an expressive-arts therapist, I want to help you tap into your inherent wisdom and creativity. By mindfully engaging in the creative process, you can develop a new understanding of who you are while learning to approach your own experiences with openness and acceptance.

If you can relate to all parts of yourself with clarity and honesty, you will be able to bring more authenticity, flexibility, and compassion to your relationships with others.

When I was going through a particularly challenging time as a young adult, I turned to creativity to help me through it. I spent hours dancing, painting simple watercolors, and writing in my journal. Creative practice focused my mind, slowed my anxious thinking, and somehow made me feel less alone.

The exercises in this book are designed to help you work through whatever you're experiencing, but they're not meant as a substitute for therapy. If you find yourself dealing with ongoing depression, anxiety, or other overwhelming emotions that impact your daily life, reach out for the support of a therapist or medical provider. My hope is that this book can offer you an opportunity to slow down, turn inward, find connection, and make meaning.

HOW TO USE THIS BOOK

This book is organized into two parts. Part I provides an overview of Mindfulness-Based Art Therapy (MBAT), including what it is, how it works, what the research says about its effectiveness, and what benefits you can expect from engaging in it.

Part II is divided into five chapters, with each one focusing on different art mediums. Here, you'll find exercises that don't require any particular artistic skill or experience and that use simple, accessible materials that you can find around your home or at a local art supply store.

You can use this book in the way that works best for you. For instance, you could work through the activities from beginning to end or choose a medium you'd like to explore and start there. The exercises in this book are about exploration and self-discovery, so engage with an open mind and know that there's no "wrong" way to do this work.

AN INTRODUCTION TO MINDFULNESS-BASED ART THERAPY

WELCOME TO PART I. In this section, you'll dive into Mindfulness-Based Art Therapy (MBAT) in more detail, investigating how and when the fields of psychology and art formally came together with the goal of increasing health and well-being while decreasing stress, anxiety, and depression. You'll learn about the benefits of engaging in MBAT as well as what the research says about how it can provide support for both mental and emotional health. You'll also learn about how to prepare for these exercises and what to expect as you begin exploring mindfulness and creativity.

What Is Mindfulness-Based Art Therapy?

Mindfulness-Based Art Therapy combines mindful awareness with creative practice. It's a way of engaging in the creative process that invites you to slow down and bring your full attention to your present-moment experience.

In the 1940s, artists, educators, and psychologists began to introduce art as a way of understanding, diagnosing, and treating illness. British artist Adrian Hill coined the term "art therapy" in 1942 while recovering from tuberculosis, when he realized that art helped him focus his mind and maintain a sense of identity separate from his illness. Around the same time, educator and psychologist Margaret Naumburg—often called "the mother of art therapy"—published several books about her use of spontaneous imagery and symbol-making with students and clients.

Jon Kabat-Zinn was one of the first to incorporate mindfulness into medical treatment. He developed an eight-week Mindfulness-Based Stress Reduction (MBSR) program in 1979, working with chronically ill patients who weren't responding to traditional treatment. MBSR has since been used throughout the world and has shown to be effective in reducing stress, anxiety, depression, and chronic pain, according to a 2017 study published in the journal *Mindfulness*.

Psychologist Laury Rappaport introduced the term "Mindfulness-Based Art Therapy" in her 2014 book *Mindfulness and the Arts Therapies: Theory and Practice*, which includes contributions from therapists, scientists, and practitioners working at the intersection of mindfulness and creative therapies. MBAT orients you toward your thoughts, feelings, and physical sensations by using creativity to communicate your inner experience when conversation is inadequate or inaccessible.

How Does It Work?

Using mindfulness and creativity to develop the skills to notice, accept, and compassionately witness yourself and your experiences is at the heart of Mindfulness-Based Art Therapy. Mindfulness asks you to bring non-judgmental awareness to the present moment, inviting you to let go of how you'd like things to be and instead accept the reality of what is. In doing so, you will begin to develop the capacity to be a witness to your experience while remaining present with it. That means that you will be able to experience your emotions while simultaneously stepping back to acknowledge and label them instead of feeling overwhelmed or consumed. Similarly, by engaging in the creative process, you will build up the courage to be present and open while welcoming the unexpected.

MBAT invites you to pay close attention to both your outer and your inner experience. This can include incorporating mindfulness practices like awareness of your breath, thoughts, and bodily sensations as you engage in drawing, writing, collage, or other creative pursuits. Because the focus is on the process, not the product, engaging in MBAT does not require any formal training in either meditation or art. How do you feel as you sit down to create? What is your experience of working with the materials at hand? What kinds of ideas and feelings emerge as you're creating? These questions can teach you as much as—if not more than—any final artistic product.

UNDERSTANDING MINDFULNESS

Mindfulness is about being fully present: paying attention to what is happening without needing it to be different.

Mindfulness meditation originated in the Buddhist tradition more than 2,600 years ago, but it has become increasingly secularized as our collective knowledge of both mindfulness and meditation has become more mainstream. It's a practice that involves tuning in to the present moment by choosing a single point of focus, whether it be the breath, sensations in the body, or—in the case of walking meditation—the physical act of walking.

While meditation denotes a formal practice such as sitting or walking, mindfulness is a quality of attention that can be accessed anywhere, at any time, by anyone. Bringing full attention to the present moment is *what* you do when you experience mindfulness, but *how* you bring that attention is equally important. Mindfulness is about cultivating curious, open, and non-judgmental acceptance of your present-moment experience, with an emphasis on kindness, gentleness, and compassion. It helps you acknowledge and accept what's happening right now, including the physical sensations in your body, the thoughts running through your mind, and the emotions you're experiencing.

With mindfulness, as with creativity, the focus is squarely on the process rather than the outcome. You're not trying to get anywhere, and there's no way to do it "right" or "wrong." By simply paying attention and observing your moment-to-moment experience with curiosity and kindness, you are practicing mindful awareness.

What Does the Science Say?

Being a compassionate and nonreactive witness to your experience is essential to Mindfulness-Based Art Therapy, and the ability to access calm yet focused states of attention and move back and forth between focused attention and open awareness can help you develop this skill. As noted in a 2016 article by Vago and Zeidan as well as a 2022 article by Weir, research has shown that mindfulness and creativity access similar areas of the brain, connecting the relaxed, open "default mode" network of the brain (which is involved with daydreaming and mind wandering) to the frontoparietal "control" network (which governs executive functioning and focused problem solving). While scientists once saw these different parts of the brain as acting in opposition to each other, we now understand that they actually work together to enhance both mindfulness and creativity.

According to neuroscientists Krass and Trantham, who contributed to the 2014 book *Mindfulness and the Arts Therapies*, combining mindfulness practice with creative expression also helps what scientists call "internal composure," or the knowledge that you have the internal resources and skills to respond to life's stressors constructively and compassionately without becoming dysregulated or overwhelmed. Internal composure aids in developing a sense of trust in yourself and your world. When faced with challenges, you are therefore better able to self-regulate, notice, and control your response, find ways to make meaning of your experience, and take time to respond mindfully rather than react.

The Benefits of Mindfulness-Based Art Therapy

When you're aware of your mental, emotional, and physical experiences and can compassionately witness them, you are equipped to respond with creativity and flexibility as the situation demands instead of simply reacting without conscious awareness.

Engaging mindfully and creatively increases self-awareness and self-regulation, and by creatively externalizing problems rather than identifying with them, you can gain insight that will increase self-compassion. In 2018, Liza Hinchey published a review of the literature on research studies done on Mindfulness-Based Art Therapy and found that study participants noted increases in self-esteem, self-acceptance, and overall well-being, as well as improved interpersonal relationships.

Creating in a mindful way helps you build an identity separate from the problems you face and offers tools to express your feelings in a meaningful way. In a study by

Heather Stuckey and Jeremy Nobel titled "The Connection Between Art, Healing, and Public Health," the authors note that using art in healing can help you shift your focus to what's going right as opposed to what's going wrong.

MBAT allows you to access your own creative insights and intuition. By cultivating mindful awareness, you will begin to trust your own ability to meet any challenge with courage and compassion.

MENTAL AND EMOTIONAL HEALTH

For their article "Everyday Creative Activity as a Path to Flourishing," Conner, DeYoung, and Silvia asked 625 study participants to self-rate their creativity, well-being, and happiness. The survey responses showed that regularly engaging in creativity correlates with greater happiness, an improved sense of overall well-being, and deeper insight into who you are and what you value. In addition, according to Hinchey's 2018 review of Mindfulness-Based Art Therapy studies, MBAT has been shown to improve the capacity to self-regulate, including the ability to notice and manage your own feelings, thoughts, and behaviors.

COGNITIVE FUNCTION

If you find your mind racing or your thinking stuck in a loop, setting aside regular time to engage in Mindfulness-Based Art Therapy can offer relief. A 2015 study by Tang, Hölzel, and Posner used neuroimaging to confirm what mindfulness practitioners have been telling us for years: Engaging in regular mindfulness practices leads to increased self-regulation, which includes the ability to control and direct your attention. Brain scans demonstrated that mindfulness practice affects the anterior cingulate cortex, the area of the brain associated with attention. Having power over your own attention allows for improved flexibility, problem-solving, concentration, and focus.

Preparing for Mindfulness-Based Art Therapy

As you prepare for the exercises in this book, it's important to find a quiet space where you feel comfortable and relaxed. Make sure you allow time for each exercise and time to transition in and out.

It's also helpful to have a ritual practice to support the work. For instance, you might engage at the same time each day, prepare a cup of tea before you get started, or take a walk after each exercise to give yourself time to integrate your thoughts, ideas, or insights.

I invite you to explore different materials in these exercises, some of which may be unfamiliar to you. Oil pastels, for example, have the consistency of an oilier crayon and can be blended or layered with other colors. Ultimately, any supplies can be substituted with what is accessible and available to you. It's also helpful to have a journal with you to answer the self-reflection questions at the end of each activity.

As you prepare, remember that mindfulness is not one-size-fits-all. Take time to see what works for you. If there is a prompt in the book that doesn't sit right or feels too overwhelming, you can engage with it in any way that feels supportive and nurturing. For example, there are several prompts to connect with your breath, but that may not feel supportive for everyone. It may be better for you to bring attention to your feet on the ground or to the sounds you hear in the room. The important thing is to tune in to the present moment in a way that honors your connection to yourself and your needs.

What to Expect as You Journey through These Exercises

The prompts in this book aim to help you become familiar with your inner world, including your thoughts, feelings, ideas, and sensations. As you work to use mindful creativity to slow down and turn your focus inward, you may feel curious, surprised, or even challenged by the exercises and what you create.

Keep in mind that it's not uncommon to feel critical of your artwork once you've finished. You may also find yourself worrying that you're failing if you don't feel completely relaxed and present in the moment. Just remember that gaining the courage and confidence to accept whatever you're experiencing is part of the process, and that there's no wrong way to do these activities.

There are a range of exercises in this book. Some of the prompts will require more time, thought, and preparation, while others can be done in just a few minutes and are meant to be approached with more curiosity and playfulness.

Using art to express and understand your inner experience will lead to increased self-esteem, confidence, and non-judgmental self-acceptance, but it does take time. Be gentle with yourself and move at the pace that feels right for you. These exercises are generally designed to be gentle and supportive, but if you feel overwhelmed or triggered, I encourage you to pause, connect with your breath, and approach your feelings with curiosity and kindness. You can reflect in your journal, step away, or share your emotions with someone you trust.

These exercises provide a space for reflection, connection, and loving insight, allowing you to be a compassionate witness to yourself and your experience.

Key Takeaways

Mindfulness-Based Art Therapy combines mindfulness with creative practice. Both mindfulness and art therapy have been shown to decrease stress, anxiety, and depression while increasing awareness, focused attention, and self-regulation.

These practices are designed to orient your attention toward what matters, develop your emotional awareness, and increase non-judgmental acceptance of yourself and your experience.

These exercises are not a substitute for therapy, so please reach out to a therapist or other medical provider if you're experiencing ongoing mental health challenges.

Throughout this book, I'll encourage you to focus on your breath and body. Feel free to modify this in any way that works for you. This could mean choosing a focus outside yourself, like listening to the sounds around you or taking breaks as needed.

Remember:

* Approach the practice with curiosity and kindness.

* Work at a pace and in a way that feels most supportive to you.

* Focus on the process, not the product.

PART II

MINDFULNESS-BASED ART THERAPY EXERCISES

WELCOME TO PART II. Here, you'll dive into exploring Mindfulness-Based Art Therapy (MBAT) using five different art mediums: painting and drawing, digital art and photography, sculpture and textiles, writing, and collage. Each chapter covers a different medium and consists of eighteen unique exercises to mindfully develop deeper self-awareness, insight, self-regulation, self-compassion, and focus. Remember to take your time and approach these exercises with openness and patience. As you become more familiar with moving through MBAT exercises, you'll find it easier to let go of expectations and outcomes, and trust that your intuition and creativity will guide you to the resources and support you need.

PAINTING AND DRAWING

As you explore Mindfulness-Based Art Therapy through the medium of painting and drawing, pay attention to your experience as you're creating, and notice how you feel as you reflect on your artwork. Remember that these exercises are meant to invite curiosity and kindness. When choosing supplies, I encourage you to use materials that you're excited to work with. Doing so not only adds to the experience of creating, but it also signals that you and your creativity are worthy of time, care, and attention. With that in mind, find what works best for you and trust that what you have will be what you need.

Paint Your Breath

Concentration
Focus
Self-regulation

PREP TIME:
5 minutes

EXERCISE TIME:
20 minutes or more

SUPPLIES
Paintbrush
Watercolor paper (or
  any rough-textured,
  non-absorbent paper)
Watercolor paints

The simple act of taking a deep breath can have an immediate and powerful impact on your mood, outlook, and well-being. This exercise brings attention to the breath, allowing the body and mind to relax while increasing focus and calm.

STEPS

1. As you begin, pause for a moment and notice your art materials. Feel the softness of your brush and the texture of the paper. Notice what colors you feel drawn to. Explore the sound of your brush dipping into the water.

2. Next, bring attention to your breath. Take two or three deep, full breaths, then let your breath find its natural rhythm.

3. When you're ready, choose a color and begin to paint along with your breath. Move the brush up as you inhale and down as you exhale.

4. Follow the breath, noticing any subtle variations and letting your brushstrokes reflect them as you move across the page.

MINDFUL REFLECTION

* Is there an image that comes to mind as you follow your breath? For instance, you might imagine your breath coming and going like a wave on the shore.

* To begin the exercise, you consciously engage your senses. How can you continue tuning in to your senses as you explore your work?

Draw the Feeling

MINDFULNESS SKILLS
Emotional awareness
Self-compassion

PREP TIME:
10 minutes

EXERCISE TIME:
20 minutes

SUPPLIES
Large paper (11" x 14")
Oil pastels or crayons

With the rush of daily life, it can be easy to ignore signals from your brain or body telling you to slow down and pay closer attention to how you're feeling. Paying attention to these signals can actually make time and space for what you need.

STEPS

1. Start by drawing a simple body outline on your page.

2. Sit quietly. Notice that you're already breathing. Place your hands on your belly and chest, if that works for you, or find another way to focus on these parts of your body.

3. Close your eyes. Notice how you're feeling. Use any sensation in your belly or chest as a clue. Do you feel any tightness? How fast is your heartbeat?

4. Taking your time, bring your full attention to whatever you're feeling and label the emotion. Imagine its color, texture, size, and shape.

5. Use the oil pastels to add this feeling to your body outline, wherever you feel it in your body.

MINDFUL REFLECTION

* Focusing on line, color, and shape, what do you see objectively in your drawing?

* What story or ideas come to mind when you look at your image?

* What title would you give your drawing?

Flow and Focus

MINDFULNESS SKILLS
Self-awareness
Self-regulation

PREP TIME:
5 minutes
EXERCISE TIME:
15 minutes

SUPPLIES
Paper
Colored pencils
 or markers

Letting your mind wander within structured limits enhances both creativity and mindfulness. This is an opportunity to explore the balance between open and directed attention, increasing flexibility and ease.

STEPS

1. Begin by drawing a large circle on your paper.

2. Starting at the top of your circle, draw a simple, continuous doodle within your circle without lifting the pen from the page, allowing your line to go wherever it wants. Pay attention to how you feel as you draw, allowing your mind and body to relax as much as possible.

3. When it feels complete, look at your free-form drawing. Notice if there is an image or figure that you can see within the overlapping lines.

4. Using different colors, complete whatever image you see in your doodle. Notice any thoughts and feelings that arise as you work.

MINDFUL REFLECTION

* What did you notice about creating a free-form drawing within the container of a frame?

* What image emerged from your free-form drawing? How does it connect to your life at the moment?

* How do you feel when you look at your completed image?

Contour Self-Portrait

MINDFULNESS SKILLS
Concentration
Focus
Self-awareness
Self-compassion

PREP TIME:
5 minutes

EXERCISE TIME:
25 minutes

SUPPLIES
Mirror
Pencil or pen
Paper

"Contour drawing" involves creating an outline of your subject, usually with a single, continuous line. The focus is on paying close attention to what you see, as opposed to how you imagine something should look. In this exercise, you are bringing this mindful attention to yourself.

STEPS

1. Sit comfortably in front of a mirror.

2. Close your eyes and take a deep breath. Bring attention to your seat and notice the support of your chair.

3. With a breath, slowly bring your hands to your face. Moving gently and taking your time, move your fingers over your face with kind attention, as if you were painting it with your fingertips.

4. When you're ready, open your eyes and look in the mirror, maintaining kind, relaxed interest and curiosity.

5. Draw your face by looking at your reflection, using one continuous line. Don't lift your pen from the page and don't worry about the end result.

MINDFUL REFLECTION

* This exercise is process-oriented versus product-oriented. How did it feel to let go of attachment to the outcome?

* How would it feel to turn this curious, kind attention toward yourself in other areas of your life?

Notice What's Neutral

MINDFULNESS SKILLS
Self-awareness
Self-regulation

PREP TIME:
10 minutes

EXERCISE TIME:
15 minutes

SUPPLIES
Pencil and paper
Oil pastels or crayons

When thinking about the past or imagining the future, it's common to overemphasize strong emotions (both pleasant and unpleasant) and their impact. This exercise directs your attention to what feels balanced, allowing for greater access to peace and relaxation.

STEPS

1. Find a quiet place to sit and take a few deep breaths.

2. As you breathe, start to notice any sensations in your body.

3. Bring your attention to any part of the body that feels neutral, calm, or relaxed.

4. Focus your attention on that neutral feeling and stay with it for at least five breaths.

5. Imagine putting this sensation under a magnifying glass. Notice where in the body you feel it, as well as its color, texture, size, and shape.

6. As you're ready, move to your paper and draw an image of this neutral sensation.

MINDFUL REFLECTION

* This neutral feeling can be subtle. What might you need to let go of to connect to what's neutral?

* If this neutral sensation could speak, what do you imagine it would say?

* How can you practice noticing and connecting to what's neutral throughout your day?

Emotional Landscape

PREP TIME:
10 minutes

EXERCISE TIME:
15 minutes

SUPPLIES
Acrylic paper
Acrylic paint

This exercise invites you to imagine your emotional experience as a natural landscape. Just as the landscape shifts and changes, so do your moods and emotions. When viewed mindfully, emotions that feel permanent and entrenched can be understood as transitory and leading you toward growth.

STEPS

1. Sitting comfortably, take a few moments to notice your surroundings, including what you can see, hear, smell, and touch.

2. Close your eyes, and begin to notice any sensations, thoughts, and feelings that you're experiencing.

3. Stay present with your emotions and notice if they shift or change over time.

4. Imagine your emotions as a landscape that you're moving through. Notice the colors, textures, sounds, and smells. How does the air feel? What's the temperature?

5. Once you have a clear image, move to your paper and begin to paint or draw this inner emotional landscape.

MINDFUL REFLECTION

* What was the atmosphere of the inner landscape that you created? Familiar and comforting? Alien and strange?

* Did the landscape shift over time?

* Can you imagine any resources or skills you might have that could help you navigate this landscape?

Protector and Protected

Self-awareness
Self-compassion

PREP TIME:
15 minutes

EXERCISE TIME:
30 minutes

SUPPLIES
Paper
Oil pastels or crayons
Journal

Feelings of worry, stress, or sadness can arise when you feel vulnerable. Though uncomfortable, these feelings can be helpful in pointing toward what you value most. This exercise offers insight into elements of your emotional life that are worth protecting.

STEPS

1. Fold your piece of paper in half.

2. Take a deep breath, noticing how your body feels and what thoughts and feelings are present.

3. Maintaining this inward focus, consider: What thought, feeling, or story is protecting me? Observe what comes up, staying connected to your breath.

4. Draw an image on the outside of the folded paper that represents this protector.

5. Now consider: What thought, feeling, or story is being protected? Notice what intuitive images or ideas arise.

6. Open your paper and draw what's being protected.

7. Take some time to journal about what you value based on this final image.

MINDFUL REFLECTION

* What do you notice about the two images you created?

* Is there a story connected to your drawings? Imagine a myth or origin story that explains them.

* What insights have you gained about your strengths and values?

Mood Music

Self-awareness
Self-regulation

PREP TIME:
15 minutes

EXERCISE TIME:
20 minutes

SUPPLIES
Watercolor paper (or
any rough-textured,
non-absorbent paper)
Watercolor paints
Colored pencils
Music player

Music is a creative resource that can enhance, amplify, or shift your mood. When approached with mindful awareness, music can act as an anchor for your attention while providing an opportunity to slow down and offer resources for self-regulation.

STEPS

1. Choose a longer, preferably instrumental song for this exercise.

2. Before you hit "play," arrange your supplies and find a comfortable seat.

3. Acknowledge how you're feeling now and imagine how you'll feel after you listen to your song.

4. Using colored pencils, draw a simple image that expresses your current mood, focusing on shape, line, and color.

5. Turn on the music. As you listen, focus on the sounds you're hearing, and notice any physical, mental, or emotional response.

6. Paint an image with your watercolors that reflects how you feel now, focusing on color, line, and shape.

7. Compare the two images and observe any differences between them.

MINDFUL REFLECTION

* Did you notice any shift in your mood before and after listening to the song? If so, how was this reflected in the images you created?

* What can you use from this experience to help manage your moods going forward?

Past, Present, and Future

MINDFULNESS SKILL
Self-awareness

PREP TIME:
5 minutes

EXERCISE TIME:
20 minutes

SUPPLIES
Drawing paper
Colored pencils or
  oil pastels

Sometimes growth can feel slow and small. Putting your present circumstances into context is an opportunity to acknowledge all the steps you've taken to get to where you are now and clarify where you'd like to go next.

STEPS

1. Fold your drawing paper into thirds vertically.

2. Check in with yourself physically, mentally, and emotionally.

3. Reflect on where you've come from and how you've arrived where you are now. Think of an image that represents your past and draw it on the top third of your page.

4. Consider where you are now, allowing yourself time to acknowledge and reflect on your growth. Choose an image to represent your present and draw it on the middle third of your paper.

5. Finally, imagine your future and where you see yourself going next. Decide what image best represents your future and draw it on the bottom third of your page.

MINDFUL REFLECTION

* Is there a connection between your past, present, and future images?

* What do you most appreciate about the steps you've taken to get from your past to your present state? How might they help you as you move into the future?

Feelings Reflection

Self-awareness
Self-regulation

PREP TIME:
15 minutes

EXERCISE TIME:
90 minutes

SUPPLIES
Circle stencils in 3 sizes
Scissors
Acrylic paint
Acrylic paper

This exercise is designed to help you mindfully discern how you're feeling and practice noticing and naming more than one emotion at a time. The process itself is an opportunity to slow down and reflect while creating a tool you can return to as needed.

STEPS

1. Make a list of emotions, such as *excited*, *angry*, *peaceful*, *sad*, *annoyed*, or *grateful*. Think of as many as you can.

2. Choose five emotions that resonate with you.

3. Decide on a color to represent each emotion.

4. Cut out three circles of varying sizes for each emotion, for a total of fifteen circles.

5. Paint each set of circles with the corresponding emotion's color. Reflect on the connection between the color and the feeling.

6. Write the emotion on the back of each circle.

7. Select any combination of three circles that best reflects how you feel, considering the size of each emotion and size of the circles you choose.

MINDFUL REFLECTION

* You can use these circles daily to check in with how you feel and notice how your emotions shift and change.

* What other emotions may be important to reflect on that you haven't included in your five?

Checking In

MINDFULNESS SKILLS
Emotional awareness
Self-regulation

PREP TIME:
5 minutes
EXERCISE TIME:
15 minutes

SUPPLIES
Drawing paper
Oil pastels or crayons

Acknowledging the impact of what's happening mentally, physically, and emotionally helps you slow down and respond, rather than react, to what needs your attention. You can do this by focusing your attention on one part of your experience at a time.

STEPS

1. Begin by pausing and connecting with your breath.

2. Close your eyes and bring attention to your body. Imagine a color, shape, or symbol connected to how your body feels.

3. Pause and come back to your breath, then notice your emotions. Label what you're feeling, then imagine a color, shape, or symbol that connects to it.

4. Return to your breath once more before checking in mentally. Notice any thoughts, ideas, or stories that come to mind. Then, imagine a color, shape, or symbol that corresponds to your mental state.

5. Finally, draw a color, shape, or symbol to represent each level of your experience.

MINDFUL REFLECTION

* Are your physical, emotional, and mental experiences connected or disconnected?

* Out of these three experiences, which is the easiest to connect to? Which is the hardest?

* Doing this exercise may have shown you that one aspect needs more attention. How can you tune in to it?

Layers of Emotion

MINDFULNESS SKILLS
Concentration
Focus
Self-awareness
Self-regulation

PREP TIME:
10 minutes
EXERCISE TIME:
45 minutes

SUPPLIES
Oil pastels or crayons
Brush with pointed end
  or pencil
Paper

This exercise encourages patience and curiosity. The aim is not to get anywhere, but rather to bring awareness to the process. You can use the colors from the Feelings Reflection exercise on page 21 that correspond to your emotions in the moment, or you can choose colors intuitively.

STEPS

1. Choose three colors that you'd like to work with.

2. Using the first color as a base, create images and shapes on the page with your oil pastel.

3. Choose your next color and layer your drawing on top of the first color, working slowly.

4. Choose your final color and add a third layer. You should have an image with three layers of color from your oil pastels.

5. Now take your pencil or the pointed end of your brush and add to your image by allowing the pencil to scratch away the layers you've created to reveal the color beneath.

MINDFUL REFLECTION

* Did you notice certain thoughts or ideas coming up as you moved through the exercise?

* This process is meant to be meditative as opposed to striving toward a particular outcome. How easy or challenging was it to stay present with each step?

Letting Go, Holding On

MINDFULNESS SKILLS
Self-awareness
Self-compassion

PREP TIME:
5 minutes
EXERCISE TIME:
30 minutes

SUPPLIES
Pencil and paper
Oil pastels or crayons

It can be difficult to decide what's worth holding on to. Feeling like you have to carry everything can become too much. This exercise invites you to imagine what you'd like to hold on to as well as what you're ready to let go of.

STEPS

1. Take several minutes to examine your hands like it's your first time seeing them. Notice how they look: Consider their texture, size, and shape.

2. Imagine that everything your hands have touched has left a mark.

3. Draw or trace the outline of your hands on the page if you are able. (If you aren't able to trace your hands, use a printout of a line drawing of two hands instead.)

4. Fill in the image of one hand with colors or images that represent what you'd like to hold on to.

5. Fill in the other with colors or pictures connected to what you're ready to release.

6. Feel free to add words related what you're holding on to and what you're letting go of.

MINDFUL REFLECTION

* How can you find ways to honor what you're holding on to in your day-to-day life?

* Reflect on ways to release what you're letting go of. You may want to tear up that piece of paper, shake out your hands, or cover over your paper with oil pastels.

Full Body Drawing

MINDFULNESS SKILLS
Self-awareness
Self-regulation

PREP TIME:
15 minutes

EXERCISE TIME:
30 minutes

SUPPLIES
Scissors
Large roll of
  butcher paper
Oil pastels or crayons

Here, you're invited to bring awareness to your body as you draw. The focus is not just on how the pastel moves across the page, but how your entire body can be a part of creating an image.

STEPS

1. Cut a piece of butcher paper that can span the width of your arms and lay it on the floor.

2. Place your hands on the paper, noticing its texture. Run your hands along the length of the paper, allowing your arms, back, and spine to engage as you move.

3. Choose oil pastels and begin to add color to your paper, covering as much of it as possible with each stroke. See if you can extend your arm across the entire page, engaging your whole body as you work.

4. Pay attention to how your body feels, as well as any thoughts and feelings that come up as you complete your drawing.

MINDFUL REFLECTION

* How would you describe the quality of your movements? Did you move gently or feel the need to push yourself?

* Can you imagine a way to move that could offer you more support or enjoyment?

Your Tree

Concentration
Focus
Self-compassion

PREP TIME:
5 minutes

EXERCISE TIME:
30 minutes

SUPPLIES
Pencil and paper
Oil pastels or crayons

Trees are majestic, ancient, and rooted. Imagining yourself as a calm, adaptable presence, unaffected by changing weather or the passing of seasons, offers many benefits. Translating this to a tangible image can be an important reminder of your stability and resilience in the face of challenges.

STEPS

1. Begin seated in meditation (or in any position that feels most meditative). Close your eyes and bring attention to the rhythm of your breath. Begin to focus on the rooted stability of your posture.

2. Call to mind a beautiful tree, real or imagined. Focus on its size, with its branches reaching upward and its solid roots anchored in the earth.

3. As you connect with the image of this tree, take your time and imagine yourself as a tree, solid and rooted but stable, flexible, and strong.

4. Notice how connecting with this image feels in your body.

5. When you're ready, draw your tree, adding roots, a trunk, and branches.

MINDFUL REFLECTION

* Trees can use complex interconnected root systems to communicate and offer one another support. What kinds of seen and unseen connections do you have to others?

* Trees develop stronger roots during storms and other challenges. How have the challenges you've faced developed your strength and resilience?

Draw a Moment

MINDFULNESS SKILLS
Concentration
Focus
Insight
Self-awareness

PREP TIME:
10 minutes

EXERCISE TIME:
25 minutes

SUPPLIES
Pencil and paper
Ruler (optional)
Colored pencils

The smallest details are often the most significant. Comics and graphic novels convey a lot of information within a limited space by focusing on the small details and moments that have the greatest impact. Doing this for yourself can help clarify what matters most to you.

STEPS

1. Consider a positive moment or memory in your life that you'd like to remember. Connect with the feeling of this moment. Where were you? How were you feeling before, during, and after?

2. Create three boxes on the page, using a ruler if you wish.

3. Draw the moment in these three panels, choosing the details that feel most significant to you. Focus on conveying the emotional impact as opposed to recreating the memory in a realistic or detailed way.

4. After finishing the three panels, create a title for the completed work and add it to the page.

MINDFUL REFLECTION

* What elements or details did you add or leave out to convey your emotional experience?

* Is there an element that you thought would be significant that you ended up leaving out?

* Looking at your finished work, what stands out as showing you what you value most?

Bird's-Eye View

Insight
Self-compassion

PREP TIME:
10 minutes

EXERCISE TIME:
30 to 60 minutes

SUPPLIES
Large sheet of paper
   (14" x 16")
Oil pastels or crayons
Ruler (optional)

It can be hard to maintain a clear perspective in the middle of a difficult situation. While you might typically be encouraged to look closer, this exercise invites you to take a wider view and recognize the bigger picture.

STEPS

1. Acknowledge your current environment. Allow yourself to mindfully notice your surroundings.

2. When you're ready, close your eyes and reflect on where you are in your life. Acknowledge how you arrived at this point and where you're headed. Consider who or what currently supports you.

3. Arrange your paper vertically and draw a horizon line about a quarter of the way from the top, using a ruler if you'd like.

4. Add a road that extends from the horizon line down the length of the page.

5. Add a shape to represent where you are along the road.

6. Add colors, shapes, or symbols to the image to represent where you've come from, who's supporting you, and where you're going.

MINDFUL REFLECTION

* Support can come in different forms. How did you visually represent the physical, emotional, mental, or spiritual support that you are receiving?

* Where did you place yourself on the road?

* What do you imagine lies beyond the borders of the page?

Feelings Conversation

MINDFULNESS SKILLS
Insight
Self-awareness
Self-compassion

PREP TIME:
5 minutes

EXERCISE TIME:
20 minutes

SUPPLIES
Drawing paper
Colored pencils

Your feelings can be viewed as messengers, though sometimes it's hard to discern what they want to communicate. By taking time to mindfully tune in and pay attention to them, you can begin to discern what your feelings are trying to say.

STEPS

1. Place a hand over your heart (if that works for you) and mindfully connect with your breath.

2. Reflect on the past week and think about the primary emotion you experienced over the last few days.

3. Draw an image to represent your emotion.

4. If this image could speak, what would it say? Add those words or phrases to the image.

5. Reconnect with your breath and ask yourself whether there is an emotion you experienced over the past week in response to the first.

6. Draw a second image to represent this second emotion.

7. Add words or phrases from the voice of this second image.

MINDFUL REFLECTION

* Are you surprised by what the feelings you drew had to say?

* Can you imagine that there are any other feelings present with something to communicate?

* Is there a feeling or voice you would like to amplify or quiet?

DIGITAL ART AND PHOTOGRAPHY

In this chapter, you'll explore Mindfulness-Based Art Therapy using photos and digital media. Taking pictures allows you to capture a moment, but it can also be an opportunity to see things in a new way. You don't need a fancy camera or tons of equipment here. Your phone or a disposable camera will do just as well. Even if you're an experienced photographer, I invite you to put your more technical equipment aside. Put the focus on the process instead of the product, giving yourself permission to be a beginner. All that's required is that you approach your environment with a sense of openness and curiosity.

Altered Photo

Self-compassion

PREP TIME:
15 minutes

EXERCISE TIME:
25 minutes

SUPPLIES
Old photographs
Scanner/copier
Scissors
Glue

Finding a photo of yourself as a child can inspire compassion for this younger self. You can offer the younger you kindness and care by connecting them to a wise figure who makes them feel safe, protected, and loved. That figure might even be *you* in the present.

STEPS

1. Find a picture of yourself as a child and make a copy of it.

2. Reflect on the image you've selected, connecting to any feelings of warmth, compassion, and care you feel toward this younger self.

3. Imagine what this younger self needed at that time.

4. Find and copy a more recent picture of you or another kind and loving presence in your life. Consider someone you know, a friend or family member, or a beloved public figure.

5. Create a new image by creatively placing the two figures together. Copy this final image.

6. Notice what thoughts, ideas, and feelings come up as you look at this new image.

MINDFUL REFLECTION

* What do you imagine the older figure in the photo is communicating to your younger self?

* How does the kind presence of a protective figure change the way you see yourself, then and now?

Love What You Love

MINDFULNESS SKILLS
Insight
Self-awareness
Self-compassion

PREP TIME:
5 minutes

EXERCISE TIME:
2 minutes per day
for one week

SUPPLIES
Camera
Journal

A person's tastes and interests can often shift under the influence of friends, family, and the culture at large. Taking time to investigate what actually sparks a personal feeling of joy, contentment, and ease allows you to cultivate more of it in your life.

STEPS

1. Take two minutes each day for a week to capture a picture of something you love. Aim to take five to ten photos total. Don't worry about censoring or explaining your choices. Instead, just notice when you feel a spark of interest, curiosity, or excitement, and take a picture.

2. At the end of the week, look at your photos and choose the three that interest you most.

3. Write down three words that describe each image, for a total of nine words.

4. Review the images and words you chose. Reflect in your journal about any insights you've gained into what brings you joy.

MINDFUL REFLECTION

* Were there any elements that came up consistently in your images, such as a setting, object, color, or mood?

* Did taking a short amount of time for yourself each day alter what you saw and where you focused your attention?

Emotional Self Portrait

MINDFULNESS SKILL
Self-compassion

PREP TIME:
20 minutes

EXERCISE TIME:
20 minutes

SUPPLIES
Camera
Personal objects
Printer (optional)

Is there a specific emotion that you'd like to connect with or express more in your life? Here, you'll take time to consider and embody that feeling. You're invited to approach this exercise with creativity, levity, and playfulness.

STEPS

1. Pause and breathe deeply. Take a moment to reflect on an emotion you want to embody.

2. Take your time in evoking this emotion and notice your physical and mental response to it in the moment.

3. Imagine what visual elements would best convey this emotion, and design a photo that includes the colors, textures, and objects that you associate with it.

4. When you're ready, take a self-portrait that includes the elements you've chosen to embody and express your emotion.

5. If you'd like, print this image and reflect on the elements that you included.

MINDFUL REFLECTION

* How did it feel in your body when taking this photo and then reflecting on the image you created?

* Consider taking a series of photos to convey different emotions. What do you imagine you might learn about yourself during this process?

The Unexpected Guest

MINDFULNESS SKILL
Self-regulation

PREP TIME:
5 minutes

EXERCISE TIME:
20 minutes or more

SUPPLIES
Camera

In the poem "The Guest House," the thirteenth-century Persian poet Rumi advises you to welcome emotions as beloved guests. This exercise extends that practice to unexpected visitors of all kinds. The intention is to develop patience, kindness, and non-judgmental awareness as you encounter and welcome anything new or unpredictable.

STEPS

1. Find a spot where you can sit comfortably for at least 20 minutes, indoors or outdoors.

2. Settle into your body and your breath, noticing how your body is feeling and bringing kind awareness to your breath.

3. After sitting for a few minutes, begin to bring your environment into your awareness, noticing the sights, smells, and sounds around you.

4. Have your camera ready to capture any guests that cross your path. This may be another person, an insect or animal, or even light. Use your imagination and focus on what you notice in your environment.

5. Take three to five pictures, capturing each guest.

MINDFUL REFLECTION

* What message do you imagine each visitor had to communicate?

* Did you notice any thoughts, feelings, or judgments coming up?

* How did you stay connected to the feeling of open, welcoming awareness?

Gentle Strength

MINDFULNESS SKILLS
Insight
Self-compassion

PREP TIME:
10 minutes
EXERCISE TIME:
30 minutes

SUPPLIES
Camera with timer
Flashlight

Working with shadows creates the opportunity to play in illusion, where the rules of physics don't apply. In this exercise, you are invited to consider ways to bring in gentleness when developing and using your strength to work through any obstacle or difficulty you may encounter.

STEPS

1. Take a few moments to find an object in your environment that can represent heaviness, stability, or strength.

2. Shine your flashlight so it casts a shadow that includes both you and your chosen object.

3. Begin to interact with these shadows, exploring ideas of gentleness and strength.

4. Notice anything that feels interesting, surprising, or unexpected.

5. Use your hands to make a final gesture of gentle strength that incorporates both your shadow and that of the object you've chosen.

6. Set the timer on your camera and take a picture of the shadow of this final gesture.

MINDFUL REFLECTION

* How did the concept of gentleness influence how you imagined expressing strength in this exercise?

* How can gentleness help you as you develop strength in your life?

* Can you imagine approaching an obstacle or difficulty with the same sense of playfulness, possibility, and ease?

Beginning, Middle, and End

MINDFULNESS SKILL
Develop mindful
    awareness

PREP TIME:
10 minutes

EXERCISE TIME:
30 minutes

SUPPLIES
Camera
Journal

Transformation is not always linear or comfortable. We often find ourselves wanting to skip to the end. For perspective and reassurance that things are moving forward, find examples outside yourself that illustrate the process of growth and change.

STEPS

1. Start outside in nature if that's available to you. Begin by noticing your thoughts, feelings, and physical sensations.

2. When you're ready, look around. Focus on sights, smells, sounds, textures, and how your body responds to them. What do you feel drawn to? What stands out?

3. Taking your time, find something that seems to be in the beginning phase of its life.

4. Next, look for something that seems to be in the middle stage of growth or change.

5. Finally, search for something that represents coming to an end.

6. Take pictures of all three subjects

7. Use your journal to write about the experience.

MINDFUL REFLECTION

* How easy or challenging was it to find something for each phase?

* What might that tell you about the transitory nature of your own personal experience?

Eye of the Beholder

MINDFULNESS SKILLS
Insight
Self-awareness

PREP TIME:
10 minutes

EXERCISE TIME:
20 minutes

SUPPLIES
Camera
Reflective surface

How you see yourself and how others see you can be difficult to discern. Everyone has their own perspective and ways of seeing. Here, you're invited to explore your physical reflection in the world around you and play with the idea of what it means to be seen.

STEPS

1. Begin with your eyes closed. Tune in to your breath and body, acknowledging how you're feeling in this moment.

2. Reflect on how you are a part of this world in this moment in time and space, connected with all the other elements, both natural and human-made.

3. As you're ready, begin to explore your space with your camera, finding surfaces or objects that show your reflection.

4. Take pictures of your reflection in various surfaces, experimenting with different light, postures, angles, etc.

5. Look through the final photographs, noticing any thoughts, ideas, and feelings that arise.

MINDFUL REFLECTION

* Imagine that each surface has its own perspective. What do these photos tell you about the different ways you may be seen?

* Consider this question: Does the reflection change the subject? Why or why not?

Sensory Adventure

MINDFULNESS SKILL
Self-awareness

PREP TIME:
5 minutes

EXERCISE TIME:
60 minutes

SUPPLIES
Camera

Exploring your environment with your senses can open up new possibilities and resources for how you understand yourself and your world. Let yourself be surprised by connecting with your senses in a new way.

STEPS

1. Begin by considering which of your senses you'll use to guide your adventure. If you can, choose a sense you don't rely on as frequently or that you wouldn't associate with photography.

2. Bring all your attention and awareness to your chosen sense. If you choose a smell, notice each smell that you're aware of. Identify what smells they are and where they're coming from.

3. Let this sense guide you. For example, allow your sense of smell to lead your adventure.

4. Once you've identified a subject that fully engages your chosen sense, take a picture of it.

5. Repeat this process, aiming to take at least five pictures.

MINDFUL REFLECTION

* What feelings did you notice coming up when relying on a sense that you don't necessarily associate with photography?

* Consider your relationship to the sense you chose. What are some other ways you can you bring more attention to this sense?

What's Inside

MINDFULNESS SKILLS
Insight
Self-awareness

PREP TIME:
15 minutes
EXERCISE TIME:
15 minutes

SUPPLIES
Junk drawer or box
  of clutter
Camera

Many people have a junk drawer, a place for all the clutter that doesn't have a clear "home." Over time, the contents can accumulate until they're over-whelming. This parallels what can happen internally with a problem that feels difficult to categorize or understand. Mindfully sorting through your thoughts and feelings can offer relief.

STEPS

1. Start by pulling out your junk drawer. Find a clear, uncluttered work surface, such as a desk, a table, or the floor.

2. Take a moment to look at the junk drawer and notice how you feel in your body and mind. Take a picture of it.

3. Empty the drawer's entire contents and begin to arrange them thoughtfully and intentionally, creating a sense of order.

4. Once every item has been put in its place, check back in with how you feel in your body and mind. Take a final picture of the assembled items.

MINDFUL REFLECTION

* Sometimes the hardest part of facing a challenge is getting started. How did you approach the process of organizing the junk drawer?

* How might you use this mindful sorting to approach challenges in your daily life?

Shift Your Attention

MINDFULNESS SKILLS
Focus and attention
Insight
Self-awareness

PREP TIME:
5 minutes

EXERCISE TIME:
15 to 30 minutes

SUPPLIES
Camera
Journal

Children are often encouraged to follow their curiosity and wonder as they explore the world around them. In adulthood, though, we're taught to block out distractions and stay focused on the task at hand. While refining your focus has its benefits, allowing yourself time to explore with openness and curiosity is equally important.

STEPS

1. Imagine you are a child between five and ten years old exploring your current environment for the first time.

2. Notice what captures your attention and take pictures from the perspective of this younger self.

3. Follow your curiosity and aim to take between ten and fifteen pictures total.

4. When you're done, take a moment to look at the pictures you've taken, noticing what you've captured as well as any thoughts, feelings, images, and ideas that come up as you look at them.

5. Take a moment to journal about your experience.

MINDFUL REFLECTION

* In following your curiosity, what drew your attention? Did you notice anything you might otherwise have missed?

* How can you use that curiosity to guide you toward understanding yourself and your values?

Find the Flaw

MINDFULNESS SKILL
Self-compassion

PREP TIME:
10 minutes

EXERCISE TIME:
25 minutes

SUPPLIES
Camera
Journal

It's easy to get caught up in labels: beautiful or ugly, good or bad, useful or useless. If you give yourself time to look beyond the surface, you may notice flaws that add to the beauty of what you love.

STEPS

1. Start outside if that's accessible to you. Take a moment to pause, noticing the air on your skin and connecting with any sounds you hear.

2. When you're ready, begin to look around. Notice what draws your attention or looks interesting. Give yourself about five minutes to let your eyes go wherever they'd like.

3. Once you've identified something interesting, get close and see what you notice.

4. Observe what makes this thing unique. Identify something that might be considered a flaw.

5. Once you've pinpointed a flaw, take a picture of what you see.

6. Give yourself time to reflect in your journal about what you discovered.

MINDFUL REFLECTION

* What was the first thing you noticed when you got close to the object of your attention?

* How did you identify the flaw? Could you give it another name?

* What can your experience tell you about how you assess flaws in yourself or others?

Path to Peace

MINDFULNESS SKILLS
Insight
Self-compassion

PREP TIME:
10 minutes

EXERCISE TIME:
30 minutes

SUPPLIES
Camera
Printer

When you're feeling upset, it's difficult to imagine how to move toward a feeling of contentment. During moments of peace, it's helpful to acknowledge the steps you took to get there. Think of it as marking the path so you can find your way back.

STEPS

1. Leave your home and visit a place in nature if that's accessible to you. Find somewhere you feel completely safe and relaxed.

2. Take a moment to explore your setting until you locate a specific spot where you feel calm and at peace. Take a picture of it.

3. Moving slowly, retrace your steps back to where you started, taking pictures all along the way.

4. When you're back at home, print your pictures and arrange them so that they track your journey to your peaceful place (that is, in reverse order of when they were taken). Imagine moving through this setting.

5. Notice what stands out to you as you look at the steps to your ultimate destination.

MINDFUL REFLECTION

* What distinguishes the journey from the destination?

* How can you find support for yourself every step of the way?

* How does knowing where you're headed guide the path you take?

Capture a Feeling

MINDFULNESS SKILLS
Insight
Self-awareness

PREP TIME:
10 minutes
EXERCISE TIME:
10 minutes

SUPPLIES
Camera
Journal

Acknowledging how you feel is the first step to understanding what's going on with you and identifying the next steps you want to take. Diving deeper into your feelings and letting them speak to you can help you become more familiar with your inner life.

STEPS

1. Take some time to connect with how you're feeling at this moment.

2. Notice sensations in your body as well as thoughts, ideas, or images that come up as you consider your feelings.

3. Find something in your immediate surroundings that represents your feeling. If you don't find something right away, keep exploring. Don't worry about what makes literal sense. Instead, use your intuition and imagination to guide you.

4. Take a picture of whatever subject represents your feeling.

5. Look at your picture and then take a moment to write in your journal from the voice of your photographed subject.

MINDFUL REFLECTION

* When you look at your picture, ask yourself what story it's telling. What does it remind you of?

* If you were having a conversation with the image you captured, what would you want to communicate?

The Heart of a Flower

MINDFULNESS SKILL
Focus and attention

PREP TIME:
15 minutes
EXERCISE TIME:
10 minutes

SUPPLIES
Camera

Flowers tend to encourage people to slow down and engage multiple senses at once. Here, you'll have the opportunity to examine one closely. You can find a flower outside in nature or buy one. It's best to choose a flower that's familiar to you.

STEPS

1. Choose your flower.

2. Start by noticing all the colors and shapes that are present in the flower you chose, allowing your eyes to take it all in. Notice feelings of enjoyment or pleasure.

3. Engage your other senses as you're ready. Inhale the scent of the flower and feel the softness of its petals.

4. When you're ready, take a picture of the flower from close range. Try to capture the heart of the flower, whatever that means to you.

5. Look at your picture and see what feelings, thoughts, ideas, or images come to mind.

MINDFUL REFLECTION

* If you chose a familiar flower, you may have had an idea of what you would find by slowing down and observing it. Were you surprised by what you noticed?

* Flowers are delicate and we tend to handle them with care. Can you imagine a way to bring this same gentle attention to other familiar objects in your life?

A Different Perspective

MINDFULNESS SKILLS
Insight
Self-awareness

PREP TIME:
10 minutes

EXERCISE TIME:
15 minutes

SUPPLIES
Camera
A familiar household
  object

It can be hard to notice the objects you use each day because they are so familiar. Taking time to mindfully observe and appreciate these simple, everyday items can provide a way to slow down and recognize all the ways that they support you.

STEPS

1. Take ten minutes to look around your home and find something that you use daily—for instance, a writing implement, a utensil, a piece of furniture, etc.

2. Once you've chosen your object, take a moment to notice its color, shape, size, and texture.

3. Recognize that someone made this object. Imagine the materials that were sourced to create it, the steps it took to get from source materials to finished object, and how you came to own it. Acknowledge how it supports and benefits you.

4. Take a picture of the object in a way that recognizes and honors its importance in your life.

MINDFUL REFLECTION

* How do small daily objects in your life connect you to others?

* How can taking time to acknowledge these connections shift your perspective about the world and your place in it?

Photo Conversation

Connection
Self-compassion

PREP TIME:
5 minutes

EXERCISE TIME:
10 minutes a day

SUPPLIES
A partner or buddy
Camera
Journal

A photo can help you express what's difficult to put into words. For this exercise, ask someone to be your partner in a daily photo exchange and notice how it feels to be in conversation without using any words.

STEPS

1. Choose someone to serve as your partner. Set an intention for what you'd like to focus on as you work through the exercise.

2. Explain that for the next week, you'll be sending one photo each day to express how you're currently feeling, and that you'd like them to respond with a photo of their own.

3. On day one, take and send a photo that connects to how you're feeling.

4. When you receive your partner's response, take a moment to look at the image. Notice what you see, imagine, and feel.

5. Send a new photo each day that reacts or speaks back to the last photo you received.

6. At the end of the week, connect with your partner and discuss the experience of sharing your images.

MINDFUL REFLECTION

* How did you decide on your partner?

* How did choosing an intention influence how you decided what pictures to take?

* Did your intention affect how you viewed the images you received?

Seeing You in Your Space

MINDFULNESS SKILLS
Focus and attention
Self-awareness

PREP TIME:
15 minutes

EXERCISE TIME:
10 minutes a day

SUPPLIES
Camera
Printer
Paper

The environments you find familiar and comforting can offer refuge and support when you need it most. At the same time, they can also tell you about who you are and what you value. This exercise asks you to look at a place that's special to you in a new way.

STEPS

1. Choose a preferred spot in your home or in a natural environment.

2. Spend time in your space and notice how it feels to be here. Take the opportunity to explore, engaging your senses as you do.

3. Take three to five pictures that capture what you love most about this place.

4. Once you have your pictures, print them out and choose one word that feels like it encapsulates each image.

5. In your journal, write down the words you've chosen in this way: "I am _____ (word)."

MINDFUL REFLECTION

* How did you determine which space was most special to you?

* What did your images and words teach you about yourself?

* If your images could speak to you, what would they say?

Pinpoint the Pattern

Concentration
Focus
Self-awareness

PREP TIME:
5 minutes

EXERCISE TIME:
10 minutes a day
for 1 week

SUPPLIES
Camera
Printer and picture
  frames (optional)

"Confirmation bias" is a term that posits that we tend to find and focus on evidence to confirm whatever perspective we already hold. Since you're likely to find support in your environment for whatever emotion you're feeling at any given moment, here you'll practice looking for the positive.

STEPS

1. Think of a particular color or shape that brings you joy and that you'd be happy to discover more often in your environment.

2. Each day for the next week, take five minutes to close your eyes and connect with your breath.

3. Open your eyes and give yourself just five minutes to find the color or shape in your environment.

4. Each day, take a picture of the color or shape in a new space, like different room or a street in your neighborhood.

5. At the end of the week, if you'd like, print and frame your photos as a reminder of where you'd like to focus your attention.

MINDFUL REFLECTION

* As the week goes on, how can you stretch your attention to take in even more of what you don't always notice?

* What qualities of this color or shape bring you joy? How else can you bring focus and attention to these qualities in your life?

SCULPTING AND TEXTILES

In this chapter, you'll find invitations to work with a range of materials through practices including simple sewing and weaving as you explore Mindfulness-Based Art Therapy using sculpture and textiles. Remember, there is no advanced skill required, and however you engage in these practices is the right way to do it. As always, the focus is on the process. Consider whatever you create as a unique reflection of you and your experience, and remind yourself that whatever thoughts and feelings arise can offer valuable insight into where and how you can develop more kindness, curiosity, and compassion toward yourself.

Create a Container

MINDFULNESS SKILLS
Focus and attention
Self-regulation

PREP TIME:
10 minutes

EXERCISE TIME:
30 minutes

SUPPLIES
Air-dry clay

Create a container to metaphorically hold whatever you're carrying either mentally or emotionally. The container acts as a reminder that you don't have to do it all or all at once. You can put things down that feel heavy or uncomfortable and come back when you're ready.

STEPS

1. Prepare your working surface by clearing a space.

2. Give yourself time to soften and mold your clay by working it for several minutes.

3. As you're working the clay, imagine a container that could hold your thoughts, worries, and fears.

4. Begin to fashion the clay into a container, working until you feel like it's finished.

5. Allow the clay to dry, placing your container in a spot where you'll see it regularly. It will serve as a reminder that you can put aside whatever you're carrying until you're ready to hold it.

MINDFUL REFLECTION

* Does the container that you created have a lid?

* How easy or difficult is it to open your container?

* Consider a regular practice of using the container as a holding place for what feels too heavy to carry, then coming back to it as you feel ready.

Weave a Memory

MINDFULNESS SKILLS
Concentration
Focus
Self-awareness

PREP TIME:
20 minutes
EXERCISE TIME:
45 minutes

SUPPLIES
Varied ribbons
  (or fabric cut into
  1" x 12" strips)
A 12" x 12" mat board
A 12" x 12" frame
Glue or tape

How you say goodbye to an experience is as important as the time you spent engaged in it. While acknowledging an ending may be complicated or uncomfortable, it also gives you the opportunity to recognize the impact of a person, place, or experience and consider how to honor it.

STEPS

1. Imagine a person, place, or thing that you want to memorialize.

2. Collect ribbons of different sizes, textures, and colors.

3. Choose twenty-four ribbons that resonate with your memory. Take your time connecting with colors and textures that evoke a certain emotion or response.

4. Once you have your twenty-four pieces, weave them together. Start by laying twelve of them next to each other lengthwise, then line up the rest horizontally. Pass each horizontal ribbon over and under the vertical ribbons in turn.

5. Once you have a final square, attach it to your mat board using tape or glue and add the board to your frame.

MINDFUL REFLECTION

* How did it feel to make intentional time and space to remember your person, place, or experience?

* How else could you make time and space to recognize and honor endings in your life?

Nature Mandala

Concentration
Focus
Self-regulation

PREP TIME:
20 minutes

EXERCISE TIME:
30 minutes

SUPPLIES
Natural materials, such as flowers, leaves, seeds, etc.

Creating in nature brings you face-to-face with the idea of impermanence. When you slow down to create something that takes intention, time, and patience with the knowledge that it won't last, you can lean into the moment and appreciate the present.

STEPS

1. Spend twenty minutes collecting natural elements in your environment. These can include leaves, shells, flowers, wood, etc.

2. Choose one of your gathered elements to be a centerpiece and place it in the middle of your working space.

3. Arrange the other elements symmetrically around the central element in a pattern of your own devising.

4. Taking your time, continue adding materials in a way that makes sense to you.

5. Notice how the different shapes, lines, and colors come together to create a cohesive whole.

6. When you've finished, take a moment to reflect on your natural mandala, then dismantle it by taking the natural elements and dispersing them.

MINDFUL REFLECTION

* Did creating something that you knew would be temporary influence how you approached your mandala?

* How does the idea of impermanence show up in other areas of your life?

* Can you imagine approaching other projects with joy for the process as opposed to focusing on the final outcome?

Me and You

MINDFULNESS SKILLS
Insight
Self-compassion

PREP TIME:
10 minutes
EXERCISE TIME:
20 minutes

SUPPLIES
Air-dry clay
Journal

Navigating relationships is a necessary and often confusing part of the human experience. Taking a moment to bring attention to a significant relationship can provide resources to consider yourself and the other person in a new way.

STEPS

1. Gather a handful of clay and begin to work with it. Notice its texture and allow yourself to give it all your focus.

2. As you're working the clay, bring to mind a relationship that has had a significant impact on you.

3. Create a simple shape or object to represent you and another to represent the other person.

4. Arrange both objects on your working surface, then add an element that demonstrates the relationship between them.

5. Give yourself some time to look at your sculpture, considering whether there's anything you'd like to add or take away.

6. Take a moment to journal about any insights.

MINDFUL REFLECTION

* How do you feel when you look at your sculpture?

* Did considering adding or taking something away shift how you felt about your sculpture?

* What insights does this sculpture give you about what you or the other person may be experiencing in your relationship?

Worry Doll

Worry dolls originated in Guatemala, where tradition states that if you whisper your worry to the doll before placing it under your pillow, the doll will present a solution overnight. Taking the time to create these dolls in a detailed and focused way offers its own comfort.

STEPS

1. Fold a pipe cleaner in half, and twist a small loop at the bend to make a head.

2. Fold both the long ends in to create arms and twist together.

3. Take a second pipe cleaner and fold in half, wrapping the bent end around the head. Fold and twist the second pipe cleaner to create legs.

4. Add fabric to create clothing for your worry doll using hot glue.

5. Optional: Whisper your worries to your doll, then place it under your pillow.

MINDFUL REFLECTION

* There's no wrong way to create your worry doll. However it turns out is the right way. What came up for you in the process of making it?

* Sometimes stating worries out loud can make them feel more manageable. What do you imagine is the best process for you to name your worries?

Visible Mending

Concentration
Focus

PREP TIME:
15 minutes

EXERCISE TIME:
20 minutes

SUPPLIES
Clothing or fabric that needs mending
Needle and thread

Visible mending is a process of repairing fabric in a way that displays the work of repair. Much like the Japanese process of *kintsugi*, where broken pottery is repaired with gold, visible mending offers an opportunity to pause and give kind attention to what needs mending in your life.

STEPS

1. Find a piece of clothing or fabric that has a small hole.

2. Choose thread that contrasts with your fabric in a way that you find beautiful.

3. Working slowly and mindfully, giving loving attention to your work, begin to sew your fabric to highlight the rip or tear. You can do this by strengthening the area around the hole with your thread.

4. Once the rip has been addressed, reinforce the material by going over it a few more times with your thread so that the mending will remain strong.

MINDFUL REFLECTION

* How did it feel to approach this exercise with a sense of loving attention?

* In a culture that values youth, innovation, and speed, engaging in a practice considered old-fashioned and slow can be challenging. How else can you practice slowing down and looking for "old" solutions to problems you may face?

Build a Cairn

Concentration
Focus

PREP TIME:
15 minutes
EXERCISE TIME:
20 minutes

SUPPLIES
About 10 rocks of
various sizes

Many cultures have used rock cairns (a carefully arranged pile of stones) to mark sacred space and serve as memorials. More recently, they have been used by travelers to signal to those behind them that they're on the right track when the path becomes harder to follow. Cairns can also serve as a reminder that finding balance takes patience, practice, and time. If doing this activity outdoors, be sure to check any laws or rules about cairns in your area.

STEPS

1. Gather stones of different sizes and shapes.

2. Starting with larger, flatter stones to form a base, stack all your stones so that they stay upright and balanced.

3. Take your time, noticing thoughts, sensations, and feelings that arise as you construct your cairn.

4. When you've balanced your stones, take a moment to look at the stack you've created and reflect on the process of creation.

MINDFUL REFLECTION

* It takes patience, practice, and time to create balance. Did you discover anything else that's necessary to the process?

* What was your primary emotion as you began your cairn? What about after you completed it?

* How can your cairn serve as a memorial or guide to others on a path that's difficult to follow?

Create Your Creature

Insight
Self-compassion

PREP TIME:
15 minutes

EXERCISE TIME:
25 minutes

SUPPLIES
Pencil and paper
Felt or other fabric
Scissors
Needle and thread
Stuffing

Examining feelings of anxiety or depression can be intimidating or overwhelming. By imagining your anxiety or depression as a creature that you're getting to know, you can bring curiosity and playfulness to the experience.

STEPS

1. Take a moment to imagine your anxiety or depression. What does it look like? If it could speak, what would it sound like? What color is it? How big is it? Make a brief sketch to capture the image in your mind.

2. Now begin to make a simple outline of your creature with your fabric. Don't worry about making this perfect; you're just getting a sense of the size and shape.

3. Trace and cut out two matching shapes, then line up the edges and sew them together, leaving a small opening. Add stuffing to give your creature shape, then stitch up the opening. Add clothing, accessories, etc., if that feels right.

4. Finish your creature and name it.

MINDFUL REFLECTION

* Now that you have a physical representation of your anxiety and depression, what do you notice? Does it change the way you feel about these emotions?

* If you could have a conversation with your creature, what would you both say?

Texture of Emotions

MINDFULNESS SKILLS
Insight
Self-awareness

PREP TIME:
10 minutes

EXERCISE TIME:
10 minutes

SUPPLIES
Paper

It can be helpful to have another way of expressing and viewing emotions other than through words alone. Using your sense of touch to tap into and communicate how you're feeling can offer unique insight.

STEPS

1. Take a moment to bring attention to your breath and body. Notice where your breath enters and the path it takes as it fills your lungs.

2. Shift your focus to your paper. Run your hands along it, experiencing its texture and size.

3. Now tune in to how you're feeling in this moment. Imagine the texture of this emotion, including its shape, size, and weight.

4. Moving slowly, begin to manipulate the paper to convey your emotion. You can fold, crumple, curve, rip, bend, or curl the page. Let your imagination and your sense of touch guide you. Keep your eyes closed if that's helpful for tuning in to your sense of touch.

MINDFUL REFLECTION

* Does your finished paper offer any clues that might help you understand how you're feeling?

* Take your time to explore the contours of your paper. Are there other feelings that come up? How are they connected to the primary emotion?

Sculpt the Dynamic

MINDFULNESS SKILL
Self-awareness

PREP TIME:
10 minutes
EXERCISE TIME:
25 minutes

SUPPLIES
Air-dry clay
Journal

You may notice that certain patterns recur throughout your life. Challenges around giving or receiving, open or closed habits of thinking, and feeling seen or unseen are all common themes worth exploring, and it's beneficial to take time to examine them in detail.

STEPS

1. Gather a handful of clay and begin to work with it. Notice its texture and allow your mind to focus completely on the material.

2. Consider a theme that's been coming up in your life.

3. When you've settled on a theme that resonates with you, begin to sculpt it. For instance, how would you create a sculpture to represent "open and closed"?

4. Once you've completed your sculpture, take a moment to reflect on what you've created.

5. Note any ideas, images, or stories that come to mind, and take a few moments to journal about any insights you've gained.

MINDFUL REFLECTION

* What pattern in your life are you responding to? Are there key details in your interactions that fit into or deviate from this pattern?

* What's the lesson that this particular theme has for you?

Mosaic

MINDFULNESS SKILLS
Concentration
Focus
Self-regulation

PREP TIME:
30 minutes
EXERCISE TIME:
30 minutes

SUPPLIES
Old cups, plates
Pillowcase
Hammer
Hard wooden or
  ceramic surface
Adhesive
Spatula
Grout
Gloves (optional)

Mosaic art dates back over four thousand years. Using small stones, tiles, or pieces of ceramic to create a larger picture requires patience, focus, and a willingness to see the bigger picture. Repurposing old ceramics that have been chipped or broken allows you to find new life in what you might otherwise throw away.

STEPS

1. Find old ceramics that have been chipped or cracked or that you no longer use.

2. Place them in an old pillowcase and knock it with the hammer to create smaller pieces.

3. When the pieces are roughly the size you want, arrange them on your wood or ceramic surface to suggest an image. You can also create a pattern, letting your intuition guide you.

4. Use your adhesive to fix your pieces in place.

5. Once the pieces are arranged, use your spatula to apply grout to any empty spaces.

MINDFUL REFLECTION

* What was it like to reuse what you already have in a new way?

* How did you navigate the steps in the process—like hammering your ceramics—in which you had limited control over the outcome?

Finding Balance

Concentration
Focus
Self-compassion

PREP TIME:
15 minutes

EXERCISE TIME:
30 minutes

SUPPLIES
Two long, thin sticks of
   roughly the same size
Flower wire
Small found objects
   (pebbles, ornaments,
   shells, etc.)
String

Mobiles combine stillness and movement, demonstrating that finding balance is about remaining steady rather than static. This practice can remind you that the best way to achieve balance is not always through force. Instead, it often requires patience and gentle practice.

STEPS

1. Lay your two sticks across each other in the shape of an X.

2. Secure the sticks together by wrapping your flower wire all the way around both of them at the point where they meet.

3. Choose the small found objects that you'd like to hang from your mobile, then attach them to the sticks using your string. You may need to use different objects or cut different lengths of string to create balanced weight.

4. Taking your time, play and experiment until you have created a balanced mobile.

MINDFUL REFLECTION

* What objects have you chosen to balance and why?

* This exercise requires adjustment and reconfiguration in order to create a mobile that can hang properly. What did you notice about the process of refining and modifying your mobile?

Familiar Dynamics Sculpture

MINDFULNESS SKILLS
Self-awareness
Self-compassion

PREP TIME:
1 minute
EXERCISE TIME:
20 minutes

SUPPLIES
Found objects in
the room
Journal (optional)

In this activity, you'll choose found objects to represent family members, friends, or other individuals with whom you have significant relationships. Approaching this exercise with a sense of openness and a willingness to be surprised can provide insight into your day-to-day relationship dynamics.

STEPS

1. Take a moment to acknowledge where you are. Look around and take in the space.

2. When you're ready, choose objects in the room to represent the significant people in your life.

3. Arrange the objects in front of you to create a sculpture that illustrates the dynamics within your family or social group. Consider qualities like proximity, size, color, etc.

4. When you're finished, take some time to reflect on the sculpture you created. What do you notice about it?

MINDFUL REFLECTION

* In addition to noting proximity between the objects, as well as other qualities like size and color, what do the objects themselves tell you about the people they represent? For instance, did you use a soft object to stand in for someone who feels more approachable?

* Looking at the sculpture, does it raise any specific questions you'd like to address with a particular family member or friend?

Wrapped Stones

MINDFULNESS SKILLS
Concentration
Focus
Self-regulation

PREP TIME:
20 minutes

EXERCISE TIME:
45 minutes

SUPPLIES
Smooth stones of
various sizes
Yarn
Hot glue gun

Binding or wrapping can be a way to handle anxiety by focusing your mind and "tying up" whatever you may be experiencing. Working with stones and yarn in a slow, methodical way allows your body and mind time to rest and reset.

STEPS

1. Choose a stone to start with. Hold it in your hands, noticing its weight, texture, and colors. Set an intention for yourself as you begin.

2. Choose one to three colors of yarn that you'd like to work with. You can use them to create a simple solid-color wrap or a multicolored weaving pattern.

3. Use your hot glue gun to attach the first section of your yarn to your stone.

4. Continue to wrap the yarn around the stone until it is completely covered.

5. When your stone is complete, attach the tail end of your yarn with hot glue.

MINDFUL REFLECTION

* This exercise invites you to work slowly and deliberately. How did you determine the style of your wrapping?

* You may have started simply and gotten more intricate with patterns and designs as you worked. How did you allow yourself to engage in this "no-fail" way of creating?

Mini Altar

MINDFULNESS SKILLS
Self-awareness
Self-compassion

PREP TIME:
20 minutes

EXERCISE TIME:
1 hour

SUPPLIES
Small wooden box
Collage images
Sequins or other
  decorations (optional)
Acrylic paint
Fabric
Hot glue gun
Small candle (optional)

Creating a small altar or shrine can be a way to honor individuals who have passed away or to celebrate revered figures in your life. Your altar can be serious or lighthearted, elaborate or simple.

STEPS

1. Spread out your materials, including a small box, images to honor the person you've chosen, and sequins or other decorations.

2. As you survey your materials, consider how your chosen subject makes you feel. What do you imagine when you think of them? Let this guide you as you decide how to assemble your mini altar.

3. Choose a background color or fabric and add it to the outside and inside of your box. Add an image of your person. Add sequins and a small candle if you wish.

4. Place your altar somewhere you will see it regularly.

MINDFUL REFLECTION

* Who in your life would most appreciate the altar you made? Consider sharing it with them.

* How can you continue to honor, celebrate, or remember the person you chose?

* Is there a specific way that you've captured the energy or style of your subject?

String Your Mala

Concentration
Focus
Self-regulation

PREP TIME:
10 minutes

EXERCISE TIME:
30 minutes (plus
an overnight
drying period)

SUPPLIES
Air-dry clay
Pencil
Yarn or small strips
of leather

Originating in India three thousand years ago, mala beads have been used for centuries to help direct focus during meditation. You can create your own as a tactile reminder to focus your mind, breath, and body throughout your day.

STEPS

1. Begin to work with the clay, taking some time to consider what you'd like to focus on to calm and quiet your mind. Set this as your intention.

2. When you're ready, take a piece of clay and roll it into a small ball, remembering your intention as you work.

3. Create between three and five small clay balls, using a pencil to pierce a hole through each one before letting them dry overnight.

4. Take your yarn or leather and thread it through each ball to create your mala.

5. You can use this mala as an anchor point, to count breaths, or to focus your attention when you feel stressed or overwhelmed.

MINDFUL REFLECTION

* What intention did you set for this exercise? How did it show up in your work?

* Focusing on the breath is not always easy. Consider using your mala as a way to focus on colors, affirmations, or counting. How does this support your focus?

Paint with Fabric

MINDFULNESS SKILL
Self-awareness

PREP TIME:
10 minutes

EXERCISE TIME:
20 minutes

SUPPLIES
Several large pieces
 of fabric
Scissors
Canvas
Fabric glue

"Painting" by arranging fabric in a three-dimensional space allows for flexibility, play, and freedom from traditional painting expectations, all of which are important as you develop tools to deal with life's challenges.

STEPS

1. Gather textiles of different sizes and colors—swaths of fabric, blankets, clothing, etc.—and find a large space where you can work.

2. Take a moment to pause, and notice any thoughts, feelings, and sensations that are present.

3. Choose one piece of fabric and cut it into a shape as if you were painting with the cloth. Notice the weight and texture of the fabric as well as its color and pliability.

4. Arrange the fabric on your canvas.

5. Cut and add other textiles as you wish, layering, arranging, and rearranging until your painting feels complete.

6. Use the glue to attach the fabric to your canvas.

MINDFUL REFLECTION

* How do you feel when you look at your final "painting"? What if you close your eyes and notice how you feel when you touch it?

* Experiment with using different surfaces, textures, and objects for your canvas. How does this change the process or outcome?

Acknowledge Accomplishments

Focus and attention
Self-compassion
Self-regulation

PREP TIME:
20 minutes

EXERCISE TIME:
30 minutes

SUPPLIES
Fabric in a variety of
  colors and patterns
Scissors
Ribbon
Needle and thread
  (or fusible webbing
  and iron)

When it seems like there are too many things going wrong to stop and recognize what's going right, it's all the more important to acknowledge and celebrate your accomplishments. It might be just what you need to keep going.

STEPS

1. Gather fabric of different colors and patterns.

2. Think back over the past week, month, or year. What are you proud of? Give yourself time and know that whatever comes to mind is right.

3. Recall this accomplishment, how you achieved it, and consider how you feel now remembering it.

4. Choose fabric to represent this particular goal or dream achieved.

5. Do the same for two to four more achievements.

6. Cut each piece of fabric into a triangle. Attach the triangles to your ribbon using needle and thread or fusible webbing.

7. Hang your banner. Whenever you see it, remember to pause and recognize your accomplishments.

MINDFUL REFLECTION

* We're often more likely to recognize someone else's achievements than our own. If it's easier, imagine that you are one of your dear friends, making this banner for you. Which of your achievements would they choose to celebrate?

* How can you recognize all the big and little ways that you show up for yourself each day?

WRITING

For this chapter, you'll explore Mindfulness-Based Art Therapy through writing. Mindful writing can help you develop self-awareness and self-compassion by expressing your thoughts and feelings in a way that creates compassionate distance, allowing you to be a non-judgmental witness to yourself and your experience. Writing also fosters insight, helping you see yourself in a new way and consider new perspectives on your own familiar story. As you engage in these writing exercises, I encourage you to practice developing a kind, compassionate voice. This new way of communicating—even with yourself—will have a profound effect on your overall well-being.

Use the First Line

MINDFULNESS SKILLS
Self-awareness
Self-compassion

PREP TIME:
5 minutes

EXERCISE TIME:
15 minutes

SUPPLIES
Pen and paper

The blank page can be anxiety-provoking for all of us. When you want to explore how you're feeling through writing, songs, poems, or sayings that inspire you can provide a little help in getting started.

STEPS

1. Choose a song, poem, or saying that has particular importance and meaning for you at this moment in your life.

2. Write down the saying or the first line of the song or poem on your page. Use this as the starting point to write your own poem along a similar theme.

3. You can repeat or alter the line as you write, letting it serve as an anchor and reference point throughout your poem.

4. Aim to make your poem at least ten lines long, repeating the first line up to three times.

5. When you are finished, reflect on how the line you chose influenced or shifted what you wrote.

MINDFUL REFLECTION

* How would the poem change if you started with a statement and shifted to a question, or vice versa?

* Using the first line of someone else's poem is like leaning on another person for support. How easy or difficult is it for you to ask for support?

Offering Forgiveness

MINDFULNESS SKILL
Self-compassion

PREP TIME:
10 minutes

EXERCISE TIME:
20 minutes

SUPPLIES
Pen and paper

When you think about the idea of forgiveness, what comes to mind? While we often think about forgiveness in the context of forgiving others, it's important to consider yourself as deserving of the kindness and compassion that come with forgiveness.

STEPS

1. Begin seated or in another position that makes you feel alert but relaxed. Make sure you feel comfortable and safe.

2. Imagine that you're asking yourself for forgiveness. What images or experiences come up?

3. Take a moment to sit with and breathe through whatever comes to your imagination. You can imagine turning toward those experiences and yourself with kindness, compassion, and understanding.

4. Now, imagine offering genuine forgiveness to the younger self that was confused or unable to act in your own best interest.

5. Write a letter of forgiveness to yourself, connecting with any feelings of warmth, kindness, and love.

MINDFUL REFLECTION

* Was there any part of you that felt that you weren't able or ready to forgive yourself? You can write a forgiveness letter to the part of you that's not ready to forgive.

* What do you need to let go of in order to offer and receive forgiveness?

Inside/Outside Control

MINDFULNESS SKILLS
Self-compassion
Self-regulation

PREP TIME:
5 minutes

EXERCISE TIME:
10 minutes

SUPPLIES
Pen and paper
Circle stencil (optional)

Taking an honest look at what you can and cannot control is often necessary when you're feeling overwhelmed. The simple act of getting things down on the page can offer a sense of relief and remind you that there's only so much within your control.

STEPS

1. Take a moment to pause in a quiet, calm place. Close your eyes if that feels safe, and take a few deeper breaths.

2. Open your eyes and draw a large circle in the middle of your paper.

3. Bring to mind an issue or task that feels overwhelming or stressful.

4. As you're ready, begin to write down words or phrases that are connected to this issue. List what is in your control on the inside of the circle and what is outside of your control on the outside of your circle.

5. When you're finished, look at your page and notice how you feel.

MINDFUL REFLECTION

* Consider getting an outsider's opinion about the list you've created. A neutral observer may have a different perspective on what you consider outside or inside your control.

* How does acknowledging what is outside your control change how you feel about the task or issue?

Conversation Between Two Parts

Insight
Self-awareness
Self-compassion

PREP TIME:
12 minutes

EXERCISE TIME:
20 minutes

SUPPLIES
Pen and paper

Imagine if different parts of you could communicate and share their stories. By pausing, tuning in, and listening with curiosity, it's possible to gain a deeper understanding of your experience and develop self-compassion and insight.

STEPS

1. Consider two parts of yourself you'd like to connect, such as your heart and your head or your hands and your feet.

2. Sit quietly and bring your attention to the first part that you'll be dialoguing with. Imagine that part of you can speak. What would it say? Begin writing from the voice of this part, taking about five minutes.

3. Shift your attention to the next part. Imagine if this part was in conversation with the first. Spend about five minutes writing from this part in response to the first.

4. Go back and forth for at least one more round.

5. When you're finished, read back over the conversation you've written.

MINDFUL REFLECTION

* How do your different parts communicate? Is it in the form of a poem, song, or story?

* Are there other parts of you that want to be a part of the conversation? What do you imagine they might want to communicate?

Describe Yourself as a Friend

Self-awareness
Self-compassion

PREP TIME:
10 minutes

EXERCISE TIME:
25 minutes

SUPPLIES
Pen and paper

Describing someone else can be easier than describing yourself without the benefit of distance and perspective. Putting yourself in the position of a kind and warm-hearted witness can give you a chance to see yourself in a new light.

STEPS

1. Bring to mind someone in your life who sees the best in you. Imagine the warmth and kindness of this person, as if they were in the room with you.

2. Now imagine that this person is describing you to a friend of theirs.

3. Begin to write out what they would say to describe you, knowing that they see and recognize your best qualities.

4. Include any stories or observations they might have about you.

5. When you've finished writing, take a moment to sit with your eyes closed, noticing how it felt to write from the perspective of a kind and loving witness.

MINDFUL REFLECTION

* What was it like to write from the position of both observer and observed?

* Developing the ability to compassionately witness yourself takes time. How can you embody this kind witnessing of others in your life and accept their reflection of you?

Draw a Card, Write the Story

MINDFULNESS SKILL
Insight

PREP TIME:
10 minutes
EXERCISE TIME:
20 minutes

SUPPLIES
Cards with evocative
images (e.g., tarot or
oracle cards)
Pen and paper

Tarot and oracle cards are becoming more and more popular, and they are sometimes even incorporated into therapy. Even if you aren't familiar with tarot, you may have cards that have evocative imagery. You can use these cards to tap into your intuition and explore the stories they can teach you.

STEPS

1. Begin by gathering and shuffling your cards, feeling their weight and texture.

2. Hold the cards and take a deep breath, connecting with any question or intention you may have.

3. Choose a card and give yourself give a few minutes to look at the image. Notice what you see, what you imagine, and how you feel as you look at it.

4. Take fifteen minutes to write down the story of the card. Use your imagination, knowing that there's no wrong or right way to go about this.

MINDFUL REFLECTION

* What did you notice about your story? Did any part of it surprise you?

* Is there any relevance or wisdom you can draw from this story that connects to your present circumstances?

* How is the story that you created a reflection of you and your life?

A Healing Haiku

MINDFULNESS SKILL
Increase calm

PREP TIME:
5 minutes

EXERCISE TIME:
10 minutes

SUPPLIES
Pen and paper

Haikus, which originated in seventeenth-century Japan, are poems that use just a few essential words to communicate an idea. Use this exercise when you don't have a lot of time but would still like to mindfully connect with and creatively explore whatever is coming up for you.

STEPS

1. Think of a situation or experience you're going through, whether in a relationship, at work, or on your own.

2. Take five minutes to write down whatever words or phrases this experience brings to mind. Don't censor yourself or worry about making sense at this point.

3. After five minutes, transition into writing your haiku. A haiku consists of three lines: the first line is five syllables, the second line is seven syllables, and the final line is five syllables.

4. After writing your haiku, give it a title.

MINDFUL REFLECTION

* What words or ideas stand out in what you wrote?

* Working within the parameters of the haiku form means you have to cut out anything that's not necessary. Is there something else that you might need to let go of—something that's not contributing to your understanding?

Narrating the Breath

Self-awareness
Self-regulation

PREP TIME:
10 minutes
EXERCISE TIME:
15 minutes

SUPPLIES
Pen and paper

Mindfulness can increase "interoceptive awareness," which means feeling and understanding sensations inside your body. Developing this sense increases your ability to give your body what it needs. The intention of this exercise is to give you an experience of mindfully tuning in and developing the vocabulary to describe your inner experience.

STEPS

1. Begin seated, with your eyes closed.

2. Focus your attention on any noises you hear, including the sound of your own breathing.

3. Follow your breath as you inhale and exhale.

4. Pick up your pen and begin to narrate the path of your breath as it enters your body until you exhale. Imagine that you're describing breathing to someone who's never experienced it. Include the way your breath feels, other sensations within the body, and any feelings, ideas, and images that connect to the experience of tracking your breath.

5. Finish writing and come back to the breath for a final minute.

MINDFUL REFLECTION

* How does narrating the breath change your experience of it?

* Consider the impact of tracking your thoughts, feelings, and sensations. How can you become a compassionate witness to your inner experience?

A Letter to Your Worries

MINDFULNESS SKILL
Self-compassion

PREP TIME:
5 minutes

EXERCISE TIME:
20 minutes

SUPPLIES
Pen and paper

In this exercise, you'll imagine that "Worry" is a person. Given time, Worry personified can tell you a lot about who you are and what you care about. Writing a letter from the voice of Worry can help you understand what's important to you and why it's worth fighting for.

STEPS

1. Imagine that Worry is sitting across from you. Notice what it looks and sounds like.

2. Write a letter to yourself from the voice of Worry, explaining what they're worried about and why. Give yourself five minutes.

3. Read the finished letter. You may be touched by Worry's care for you or amused by Worry's fears.

4. Take five minutes to write a response. You can thank Worry for their concern and explain why their fears are unfounded, or you can explain why you plan to continue despite their fears.

5. When you're finished, find a way to release Worry by safely discarding the letter.

MINDFUL REFLECTION

* Did the voice of Worry sound familiar to you? Do you imagine it has been influenced by someone else in your life?

* In your response letter, what reassurances did you provide as evidence of your ability to persevere despite Worry's influence?

Collage Poem

MINDFULNESS SKILL
Insight

PREP TIME:
20 minutes

EXERCISE TIME:
15 minutes

SUPPLIES
Old magazines
  or newspapers
Scissors
Paper and
  glue (optional)

When you can't find the right words to describe what you're trying to express, you can use words you find in old magazines or newspapers as a starting point.

STEPS

1. Collect old magazines or newspapers that you're willing to cut up.

2. Give yourself about ten minutes to look through your old media and rip out pages with text that catches your eye. Don't spend too much time reading or getting pulled into the actual content.

3. Spend ten minutes cutting out words and arranging them in a pile.

4. Take a moment to sit and breathe.

5. As you're ready, choose words and put them together into phrases, beginning to make a poem. Don't censor yourself.

6. When you've finished, look at the completed poem and read it aloud.

7. You can glue your completed poem to a piece of paper if you choose.

MINDFUL REFLECTION

* Was there a connecting or unifying theme to the words you chose?

* What was the overall emotion or tone of your poem?

* How did having the words pre-selected influence your experience?

Hero of Your Story

MINDFULNESS SKILL
Self-compassion

PREP TIME:
10 minutes

EXERCISE TIME:
20 minutes

SUPPLIES
Journal
Movie soundtrack
Music player
Pen

Here, you'll imagine that you are the protagonist of a story you're telling yourself. Looking at your life so far, how would you describe your greatest accomplishments? You're invited to tell the story in the context of your heroism, courage, and fearlessness in overcoming the obstacles and challenges you've faced.

STEPS

1. Sit down with your journal in a comfortable spot. Begin to imagine your life as if it were being played out on a giant screen in front of you, with each moment accompanied by a movie soundtrack that adds emotional resonance.

2. Play the movie soundtrack in the background. Choose one song that resonates with an emotional moment in your life.

3. Once the music has ended, write the scene of your greatest accomplishment.

4. Read it back to yourself while playing the music and notice how you feel.

MINDFUL REFLECTION

* How does the music you chose influence your perception of what you accomplished?

* Why was this accomplishment meaningful for you?

* How can you contextualize this moment in a way that impacts your current and future view of yourself?

Voice of the Past

MINDFULNESS SKILL
Insight

PREP TIME:
20 minutes

EXERCISE TIME:
25 minutes

SUPPLIES
Old journals or writing
Pen and paper

The practice of journaling gives you a record and a window into how you were feeling and what you were thinking at a given moment in time. Journals often provide wisdom that you can return to when you need it most.

STEPS

1. Gather old journals or other writing that you've done.

2. Take a moment to reflect on where you were, how you felt, and what was happening in your life at the time of the writing. Offer warmth, kindness, and compassion to this younger self.

3. Begin to read over your writing. Make note of anything that stands out to you.

4. Imagine that this younger self has a message to communicate. What is it?

5. Take twenty minutes to write, keeping your pen moving and coming back to the words and phrases you noted if you get stuck.

6. When you've finished writing, read back over what you wrote.

MINDFUL REFLECTION

* How did it feel to find inspiration from your own earlier writing? Are you surprised by what you found?

* What message stands out to you from what you wrote?

* What other messages from your past may be worth revisiting?

Imagining Support

MINDFULNESS SKILLS
Self-awareness
Self-regulation

PREP TIME:
5 minutes
EXERCISE TIME:
15 minutes

SUPPLIES
Large paper
Oil pastels or crayons

Consider how you currently support yourself in challenging circumstances. For this exercise, you'll allow your intuition and creativity to influence how you answer this question. You'll also experiment with using your non-dominant hand to open up different and possibly surprising possibilities.

STEPS

1. Begin by sitting quietly. Close your eyes if that feels right to you.

2. Take a breath and ask yourself, "What do I need for support right now?" Notice what images and ideas come to mind.

3. Pick up an oil pastel with your non-dominant hand. Begin to write your response.

4. Feel free to write large or small letters, and pay attention to the dynamic of moving your hand.

5. When you're done, take some time to take note of what you wrote. See if there is one thing you can begin to do right now to offer yourself support.

MINDFUL REFLECTION

* Was there anything you wrote that feels surprising or resonant?

* How can you incorporate more practices of self-care and support, starting today?

* What expectations can you let go of about how something needs to be done in order to provide support?

A Kind Word

MINDFULNESS SKILL
Self-compassion

PREP TIME:
10 minutes

EXERCISE TIME:
20 minutes

SUPPLIES
Journal
Pen

How you talk to yourself can influence how you think, feel, and act. Speaking to yourself in a way that would encourage a beloved friend or family member can help you imagine offering yourself a sense of calm, peace, and support.

STEPS

1. When you're ready, find a quiet place and get comfortable.

2. If you've been speaking to yourself in an unkind way, begin to imagine words that would be more kind and encouraging.

3. Choose up to three phrases that you'd like to start affirming to yourself. For example: *You're doing your best, I'm proud of you,* or *Thank you.*

4. Write each phrase down ten times, taking your time and repeating it to yourself as you write.

5. Read each phrase out loud, noticing your thoughts and feelings as you hear the words.

6. Take a moment to sit quietly and breathe slowly, repeating the words to yourself.

MINDFUL REFLECTION

* What do you imagine is the benefit of speaking to yourself in a harsh way? Is there a cost?

* Can you imagine that there's a benefit in speaking to yourself in a kind or compassionate way?

* How can you practice speaking kindly to yourself?

Ask the Question

MINDFULNESS SKILLS
Insight
Self-compassion

PREP TIME:
10 minutes

EXERCISE TIME:
20 minutes

SUPPLIES
Timer
Journal
Pen

Asking a question and being open to the answer requires letting go of what you imagine the answer is, or what you think the right answer should be. You can make time here to write past the inner censor until you come to a place of openness and possibility.

STEPS

1. Sit quietly and comfortably.

2. Allow a question to come to your mind.

3. When you're ready, set your timer for ten minutes and begin writing in your journal.

4. Start with your question, then keep writing without lifting your pen from the page. It doesn't need to make sense. Write whatever comes to mind, don't worry about filtering yourself, and keep breathing.

5. If you get stuck, write your question again and keep going.

6. After ten minutes, stop writing and notice any sensations in your body as well as what you're thinking and feeling.

7. Read back over your writing and see what stands out.

MINDFUL REFLECTION

* What words, phrases, or images feel significant to you? You can do more writing using this as a starting point.

* Writing past your inner critic or censor takes practice. How can you continue to develop a practice of working past that?

Discerning the Message

MINDFULNESS SKILLS
Concentration
Focus
Insight

PREP TIME:
10 minutes

EXERCISE TIME:
15 minutes

SUPPLIES
Old book you don't
  mind altering
Black marker

Figuring out what is worth taking in and what should be filtered out can be challenging. This is especially true in our digital age, when the ability to respond quickly can give communication a sense of immediacy. This exercise is a practice in eliminating whatever isn't absolutely necessary.

STEPS

1. Sit with the book on your lap, eyes closed, feeling its weight as you breathe slowly.

2. When you're ready, open the book, noticing the words with soft eyes.

3. Choose a page to work with and begin to read more closely.

4. Underline the first word that resonates.

5. Use your marker to cross out all the words on the page before it.

6. Scan until you find what you feel should be the next word, then black out the words between.

7. Move through the entire page until you've strung together a sentence of chosen words, blacking out the other words on the page.

MINDFUL REFLECTION

* How did it feel to narrow your focus to only those words that matter to you, actively covering over words of less importance?

* How else can you non-judgmentally decide what's unnecessary and block it out?

Turning Thoughts Into Poetry

MINDFULNESS SKILL
Self-awareness

PREP TIME:
15 minutes

EXERCISE TIME:
20 minutes

SUPPLIES
Journal
Pen

Allowing yourself to simply be in the present moment and notice your experience is a skill that can be used in every area of your life. Becoming more aware of your physical, mental, and emotional state requires a willingness to notice without judgment.

STEPS

1. Begin by sitting comfortably and checking in with how you're doing physically and emotionally. Notice what's on your mind, acknowledging both the content of your thoughts as well as their context. Is your thinking spacious or crowded, fast or slow?

2. After sitting calmly and noticing your experience, shift your attention to your journal.

3. Give yourself ten minutes to write freely. Keep your pen moving on the page and allow your intuition to direct your writing.

4. Take a few minutes to review your writing, highlighting words and phrases that stand out to you.

5. Take five minutes to write a poem based on your highlighted words.

MINDFUL REFLECTION

* Quieting the inner critic of self-judgment takes time. Did you notice how you were able to step back and notice your critical voice instead of reacting to it?

* How can you bring this spirit of kind attention to other areas of your life?

Write Your Future

Self-compassion

5 minutes

20 minutes

Pen and paper

Writing about your past can be cathartic and healing. Writing about your future is an act of courage and defiance. Take time to imagine the best possible future for yourself, understanding that you can use your imagination to visualize either the worst or the best.

STEPS

1. Sit mindfully and tune your attention to your body, feelings, and thoughts.

2. Become conscious of thinking your thoughts in addition to observing them.

3. As the witness, begin to tell the story of your future.

4. Write about your future for twenty minutes, using the present tense to describe where this future self is, who is in your life, and how you are feeling. Include details that are meaningful to you.

5. You can keep this writing reflection and refer to it occasionally as a way of directing your energy and focus.

MINDFUL REFLECTION

* How did it feel for you to write about the future in the present tense?

* You can turn to this mindful exercise at different times in your life as a way of checking in with your future self and sending positivity and encouragement.

CHAPTER

five

COLLAGES

For this chapter, you'll be working with collage, a medium in which you'll use found images—for example, from magazines, postcards, posters, old books, or the internet—to create your art. I encourage you to gather an ongoing collection of images that inspire, challenge, or intrigue you. It's helpful to have a wide variety of images to choose from and to consciously consider how the images you select reflect the diversity you experience in everyday life. You may need to actively seek out diverse images, but it'll be worth it to have pictures that represent the vast and varied spectrum of human experience.

Your Home

PREP TIME:
5 minutes

EXERCISE TIME:
15 minutes

SUPPLIES
Collage images
Scissors
Glue
Paper
Journal

Consider what makes a space a home. A house, apartment, or other dwelling can represent a place of support, stability, and rest, a retreat from the outside world. Consider what qualities are needed for you to feel stable, supported, and at peace as you create your home.

STEPS

1. As you begin, consider what an ideal home would be for you. Imagine colors, textures, and the feeling of being in this space.

2. Look through your collage images and pull out any that connect to your feeling of home.

3. Once you have a collection of images, take a moment to sit back and breathe.

4. When you're ready, begin sifting through the images until you find the ones that resonate most with you.

5. Glue your final images on the paper, suggesting the shape of a house.

6. Take some time to write in your journal and reflect on the images you've chosen.

MINDFUL REFLECTION

* What are three words that describe the vibe of your ideal home?

* How are those characteristics present in your life right now?

* Does your image reflect any ways you can start connecting with these qualities as they currently exist in your life?

Values

MINDFULNESS SKILL
Self-awareness

PREP TIME:
10 minutes

EXERCISE TIME:
25 minutes

SUPPLIES
Collage images
Scissors
Glue
Paper

One benefit of mindful awareness is the increased happiness that comes with clarifying and acknowledging what matters. Taking the time to create a tangible reflection of your personal values can help you stay connected and aligned with what feels most important to you.

STEPS

1. Take a moment to sit quietly and reflect on what's most important to you at this moment. What do you value?

2. As you're ready, begin to look through your images until you find something that reflects what matters most to you.

3. Continue looking through your images until you have seven to ten images that speak to your values, then glue them to the paper.

4. Once you've completed your collage, take a moment to reflect on and write down the values that the images represent for you.

MINDFUL REFLECTION

* After devoting time to reflecting on and listing what matters to you, take some time to consider how you are currently living in alignment with your values.

* Do you have a value that needs more attention right now? How can you bring more focus to it?

Acknowledging Your Roots

MINDFULNESS SKILLS
Self-awareness
Self-compassion

PREP TIME:
15 minutes

EXERCISE TIME:
20 minutes

SUPPLIES
Pencil and paper
Collage images
Journal (optional)

Here, you'll consider the connection between your physical self and what keeps you grounded and connected to your roots. Your roots may you connect you to a culture, a family, a place, or even the world.

STEPS

1. Draw a horizontal line in the middle of your paper that represents the ground. Close your eyes, breathe, and imagine standing on it.

2. Now imagine a line connecting you to the earth and your ancestors, acknowledging that you weren't born knowing how to move through the world and that you were taught. Consider what supports you and provides metaphorical balance and stability.

3. When you're ready, find images to represent your roots. Place them on your paper below the line.

4. Find an image or images to represent you. Place them above the line.

5. Glue the images to your paper.

6. Reflect on the completed collage in your journal.

MINDFUL REFLECTION

* What's the quality of the roots in your image?

* Do your roots connect you to a particular person, community, or place?

* What has developed or strengthened your roots over the years?

* What do your roots need to feel healthy and supported?

Alebrije-Inspired Animal Guide

MINDFULNESS SKILL
Insight

PREP TIME:
10 minutes

EXERCISE TIME:
25 minutes

SUPPLIES
Collage images
Scissors
Glue
Paper

Alebrijes are folk-art sculptures of mythical animals that represent spirit companions and guides. They originated in Mexico and often include features of more than one animal, such as a horse with wings. Consider which animal characteristics resonate most with you as you make your own alebrije-inspired collage.

STEPS

1. Find images of different animals and lay them out in front of you.

2. Closing your eyes, take a moment to connect with your breath and body.

3. Ask yourself, "What animal has something to teach me?" Give yourself a moment to sit with the question and the answer.

4. As you're ready, open your eyes, and find the animal images that most inspire and call to you.

5. Cut out the images and fashion your own magnificent animal creature with all the qualities that you most admire.

6. Glue the images to your paper to form a completed alebrije-inspired collage.

MINDFUL REFLECTION

* What message do you imagine your alebrije would communicate?

* What qualities and characteristics of your alebrije would you like to embody in your life?

* Reflect on how you already possess certain characteristics of your alebrije-inspired collage. What are they?

Contrast Collage

MINDFULNESS SKILLS
Insight
Self-compassion

PREP TIME:
10 minutes

EXERCISE TIME:
20 minutes

SUPPLIES
Collage images
Paper
Glue

Getting to know your anxiety and depression is important, but it's equally important to connect to what offers relief. Take some time to consider what qualities are present in your daily life, as well as what their opposites would be.

STEPS

1. Sit comfortably and close your eyes if that feels safe. Check in with how you're feeling physically, mentally, and emotionally.

2. Consider how you've been feeling over the past week.

3. Look through your images and find three to five pictures that express how you've been feeling. Set them aside.

4. Return to your present feeling of neutrality or calm.

5. Now choose three to five images that express a contrast with your first set, and set them aside.

6. Assemble all your images and attach them to your paper.

7. Reflect on your completed collage, noticing the contrast and similarities among the images.

MINDFUL REFLECTION

* What does the contrast among the images tell you about your emotions?

* Take a moment to reflect on how it would feel to embody an emotion and its opposite. Is there a way to find more balance based on the pictures you've chosen?

Calm Cards

SUPPLIES
Collage images
Index cards
Glue
Lamination materials
   (optional)

Words have personal meaning, and taking time to understand what "calm," "peace," or "balance" mean to you can help you cultivate those qualities. Identifying what you need and exploring associated images can be a good place to start.

STEPS

1. Gather your collage images and take some time to take in the shapes, lines, and colors. Notice how you feel in your body as you look.

2. As you're ready, begin to choose images that elicit a positive feeling.

3. Choose three feelings or sensations that are supportive or soothing to you. For example: peace, calm, and balance.

4. Create an index card for each of the feelings you've chosen, selecting images that connect to each one and attaching them to a card.

5. Write the feelings on the back of the cards, including any words of encouragement.

6. Laminate your cards if you would like to.

MINDFUL REFLECTION

* What did you discover about your personal definition of "calm," "peace," or "balance" in this exercise?

* Are these definitions different from what you imagined or assumed they would be?

* How can you continue to develop and refine the meanings of these words for yourself?

Creative Reuse

MINDFULNESS SKILL
Self-compassion

PREP TIME:
12 minutes

EXERCISE TIME:
30 minutes

SUPPLIES
Old artwork
Scissors
Glue
Large paper

You can collage with art you've already made, putting different pieces together to make an entirely new creative work. If you're hesitant to cut up your old art, choose something you're ready to let go of and remember that your artwork is being transformed, not discarded.

STEPS

1. Take some time to look through your completed artwork and notice how you feel as you reflect on your work.

2. Taking your time, choose a few images that you're ready to transform into something new.

3. Moving slowly and mindfully, begin to cut up your old artwork. Notice the colors, shapes, and lines that emerge in these new pieces.

4. When you're ready, take the cut-up pieces of your original artwork and begin to collage a new, unified piece by gluing them onto your paper.

5. Reflect on your finished piece and give it a title.

MINDFUL REFLECTION

* Did transforming your work into something new highlight or emphasize anything that you may have missed before?

* What juxtapositions surprised, inspired, or delighted you?

* How can you imagine transforming something in your life that you're ready to see in a new way?

Negative Space Self Portrait

Insight
Self-awareness

PREP TIME:
15 minutes
EXERCISE TIME:
25 minutes

SUPPLIES
Selfie
Printer
Collage Images
Paper
Glue

Consider what people would see if they could understand what was going on with you internally. Imagine how they would respond if you could show them what you care about most.

STEPS

1. Choose a selfie that reflects how you see yourself. Resize it to fit a letter-size sheet of paper, then print it out.

2. Think about which of your five senses you connect with most strongly. Choose images to represent what you would like to see, smell, taste, hear, or touch in the world, then attach them to the part of your image that corresponds with that sense. For example, if you'd love to see more calm and beauty, find pictures that represent that for you and consider gluing them onto your eyes. If you're exploring the sense of touch, it can be empowering to think outside the box.

3. Take your time, give yourself permission to be creative, and know that you can't do this wrong.

MINDFUL REFLECTION

* Were the images that you chose connected or far-ranging?

* Is there a clue in the final image as to what is most important to you?

* What's the story of the person captured in your final image?

Complete the Story

MINDFULNESS SKILLS
Self-awareness
Self-regulation

PREP TIME:
10 minutes

EXERCISE TIME:
15 minutes

SUPPLIES
Collage images
Oil pastels or crayons
Paper
Glue
Journal

When you can't see the whole picture, you have an opportunity to fill in the blanks. Whether the details you add are helpful or harmful is often up to you. Try creating a story that nourishes you.

STEPS

1. Gather your collage images and sift through them until you find an image that seems to tell a greater story.

2. Look at your chosen image and see what story emerges. Take your time to imagine a story that includes details that are supportive, comforting, and soothing.

3. As you're ready, begin to expand on the image using other collage images and oil pastels.

4. Continue working until you have a complete image that tells a nurturing and restorative story.

5. Take a moment to write in your journal about the story and your experience of filling it with supportive details.

MINDFUL REFLECTION

* How easy or difficult was it to tell a comforting story?

* How do you feel when you look at your completed image?

* What does this exercise tell you about the power you have to tell your story in the way that is most meaningful to you?

Reflection

MINDFULNESS SKILL
Insight

PREP TIME:
10 minutes

EXERCISE TIME:
20 minutes

SUPPLIES
Collage images
Paper
Glue

This exercise is designed to help you tune in to your inner voice, and it works best if you follow the instructions step-by-step instead of reading all the way through them before you begin. This helps with quieting the inner critic and allows you to be surprised by your discoveries.

STEPS

1. Collect your collage images and lay them out in front of you. Notice how you feel as you look at the images and take a deep breath.

2. Run your hand over the pictures, then choose five that you feel drawn to and set them aside.

3. Create a collage with your five images, arranging them on the page however you like.

4. Choose a word that corresponds with each image.

5. Write your words on the back of the paper in this format: "I am_____."

MINDFUL REFLECTION

* Do the words you chose correspond to qualities that you recognize in yourself or that you would like to cultivate?

* How do these images help point you toward the attributes that you would like to embody in your life?

Tissue Paper Collage

MINDFULNESS SKILLS
Concentration
Focus
Self-regulation

PREP TIME:
10 minutes
EXERCISE TIME:
30 minutes

SUPPLIES
Tissue paper in a
  variety of colors
Glue
Paintbrush
Paper

Tissue paper is delicate and forgiving. You can work with this material with curiosity and playfulness, understanding that there's no wrong way to do this exercise.

STEPS

1. Gather tissue paper of different colors. Explore the paper with your senses, noticing its color and texture.

2. Choose a color you'd like to start with, then tear off a piece of the tissue paper and "paint" it onto your page using glue and your paintbrush to attach it however you like.

3. Continue adding tissue paper in different colors in any way that interests you. Experiment with layering, texture, size, and placement.

4. Keep going until you feel you've reached a good stopping point.

5. Complete your piece by covering the entire page with glue to seal it. Just remember to rinse out your paintbrush right away so it doesn't dry with the glue.

MINDFUL REFLECTION

* How did the medium of tissue paper influence your experience of making this collage?

* How did it feel to work in this way?

* How did your experience of creating this collage connect to how you encounter new or unexpected situations?

Peaceful Place

Self-awareness
Self-regulation

PREP TIME:
12 minutes

EXERCISE TIME:
20 minutes

SUPPLIES
Collage images
Paper
Glue

Using your imagination to provide comfort and support is a skill worth developing. In moments of distress, imagining a special place can give you a much-needed sense of feeling grounded and calm.

STEPS

1. Bring awareness to your body by sitting or lying down in a comfortable position and allowing yourself to relax.

2. In this relaxed state, imagine that you are in a special place where you feel completely at peace.

3. As you're ready, begin looking through your collage images to find pictures that remind you of this sense of serenity.

4. Choose as many pictures as you'd like and attach them to the page in any configuration that speaks to you.

5. When you've finished, return to your comfortable seated or lying-down position. Imagine you are back in your special place, taking time to imagine how it feels to be there.

MINDFUL REFLECTION

* Based on your experience of imagining this special place, which of your senses are connected to your sense of peace?

* Is there anything from your experience or image that you can bring into your space to help you feel more serene?

Beneath the Surface

MINDFULNESS SKILLS
Insight
Self-awareness
Self-compassion

PREP TIME:
5 minutes

EXERCISE TIME:
25 minutes

SUPPLIES
Paper
Oil pastels or crayons
Collage images
Glue

While you may have things about yourself that you keep private, connecting with others does invite you to share who you are in ways that feel safe and comfortable. This exercise helps you imagine what parts of yourself you'd like to share.

STEPS

1. Begin by reflecting on your week and acknowledging any interactions with others.

2. Position your paper vertically. Draw a horizontal line about a quarter of the way down the page.

3. Draw an image that represents an iceberg, with the majority taking up the bottom three-quarters of the page and the rest above the horizontal line.

4. Place collage images representing the parts of yourself that you show to others above the line, and place images representing the parts you keep hidden or private beneath the line.

5. As you reflect on your final image, notice how you feel. Imagine what it would feel like to lower the line even a small amount.

MINDFUL REFLECTION

* What is something you've been keeping to yourself that you'd like to share? Who would you like to share it with?

* Is there anything below the line that feels central to who you are? Can you imagine how sharing might help you feel seen?

Your World

MINDFULNESS SKILL
Insight

PREP TIME:
10 minutes

EXERCISE TIME:
25 minutes

SUPPLIES
Paper
Pen or pencil
Collage images
Scissors
Glue

It can often be challenging to decide where to focus your energy with so many things vying for your attention. Imagine constructing your world based on what you value most and where you'd like to place your resources and time.

STEPS

1. Begin with a blank piece of paper. Draw a large circle on the page.

2. Place your hands on the paper and take a deep breath.

3. Begin to sift through your collage images, noticing what you find interesting, important, inspiring, or beautiful.

4. Set aside your images and use your scissors to fit them inside the circle you've drawn on the page. Imagine that this represents your world and all you'd like to see in it.

5. Take your time and fill in the entire circle.

6. When you've finished, reflect on your collage world and what's included in it.

MINDFUL REFLECTION

* What do you notice that's included and left out of your final image?

* Is there anything you'd like to add or take away?

* Choose one part of your collage to focus on even more closely. Where would you like to place your attention right now?

Color Collage

MINDFULNESS SKILLS
Concentration
Focus
Self-regulation

PREP TIME:
5 minutes
EXERCISE TIME:
30 minutes

SUPPLIES
Collage images
Scissors
Paper
Glue
Journal (optional)

Take time to consider the colors that are most peaceful or stress-inducing for you. Noticing how colors influence your mood can help you identify and seek out soothing resources when you need them most.

STEPS

1. Notice what colors you have in your home environment. Choose one color that invokes feelings of peace, calm, or happiness for you.

2. Look through your collage images to find sections that feature this color, and cut them out.

3. Begin to form a color collage. Your chosen color can be placed wherever you like, or you can create a pattern. For example, you could move from dark to light.

4. Cover your paper completely with your chosen color. Notice how you feel when you look at it.

5. If you like, take a moment to reflect in your journal about the thoughts, feelings, and sensations you associate with this color.

MINDFUL REFLECTION

* Is there a color that you are often drawn to? Is there a color you can't stand?

* What characteristics do you associate with the color you chose?

* How can you use this knowledge to help you going forward?

Relaxed and Supported

MINDFULNESS SKILL
Self-compassion

PREP TIME:
5 minutes

EXERCISE TIME:
15 minutes

SUPPLIES
Collage images
Scissors
Paper
Glue

This is an invitation to move very slowly and gently. Imagine how you can convey the essence of what you'd like to express with as little effort and work as possible.

STEPS

1. Begin in a comfortable position for working on your art. Notice your spine and connect to feelings of both support and relaxation.

2. Close your eyes and take a few deep breaths.

3. Notice what thoughts, images, and feelings come up as you connect with your spine and your relaxed yet supportive posture.

4. Choose collage images that connect with this feeling, then arrange them on the page.

5. As you're working, try to choose the simplest way to convey this feeling. Your collage may consist of only one or two colors, shapes, or pictures.

6. Once you determine the simplest form of your feeling, glue your images to the paper.

MINDFUL REFLECTION

* What were you able to let go of in order to get to the final simple image?

* How can you connect with more gentleness and ease in other areas of your life?

Collage Your Day

Insight
Self-awareness
Self-compassion

PREP TIME:
15 minutes

EXERCISE TIME:
15 minutes

SUPPLIES
Collage images
Glue
Paper

Your day may have many ups and downs that affect how you feel. Acknowledging what remains constant—such as your breath, your body, and your perseverance—is invaluable. Create a visual representation of your day using collage and include this constant as the throughline.

STEPS

1. Reflect on your day: what happened, how you responded, and your thoughts and feelings.

2. Choose three to five collage images to visually represent elements of your day.

3. Arrange and glue your images to your paper in an order that represents your day from beginning to end.

4. Choose an image, shape, or color to represent the throughline of your presence.

5. Collage this image, shape, or color as a continuous line from one side of your paper to the other. For example, you can create a pink line that represents you and attach one continuous pink piece or connect several smaller pink images.

MINDFUL REFLECTION

* Aside from your presence, what is a throughline or constant for you throughout the day?

* Does the color or image you chose to represent yourself correspond, complement, or contrast with the images that represent your day?

Find the Metaphor

MINDFULNESS SKILLS
Insight
Self-awareness

PREP TIME:
10 minutes

EXERCISE TIME:
30 minutes

SUPPLIES
Collage images
Scissors
Glue
Paper
Journal

Using a metaphorical image, symbol, or story to describe an issue can be helpful for gaining a new perspective and providing deeper understanding of what you're going through. A visual metaphor can often communicate what words can't.

STEPS

1. First, take a few moments to consider a challenge you're currently facing. Assess the objective facts: who or what is involved? Then consider what story, symbol, or image comes to mind when you think about this situation. What does it remind you of?

2. Take a few minutes to look through your collage images for ideas and inspiration.

3. When you find pictures that connect to a metaphor for how you imagine this situation, arrange them on the paper to convey the idea, image, or story.

4. Take your time in finalizing and gluing down your images.

5. Take a few minutes to describe the metaphor in your journal as well as how it applies to your current situation.

MINDFUL REFLECTION

* How does the metaphor you chose add to your understanding of the challenge you're facing?

* Has this exercise given you new insights into how you might address this challenge?

RESOURCES

Books

Comfortable with Uncertainty is a collection of talks given by the Buddhist nun Pema Chödrön. She details ways to find peace and balance in the midst of discomfort and uncertainty.

Mindfulness and the Arts Therapies: Theory and Practice, edited by Laury Rappaport, PhD, details early insights, explorations, and interventions of pioneers in the field of MBAT.

The Mindful Path to Self-Compassion: Freeing Yourself from Destructive Thoughts and Emotions, by Christopher K. Germer, PhD, provides practices, prompts, and research related to developing self-compassion through mindfulness.

Podcast

The Mindful Psychology Podcast is hosted by Geneviève Angela B. and features guests from around the world exploring mindfulness, psychology, neuroscience, and holistic health.

Therapy

Npr.org/lifekit is a free podcast providing life advice on a range of subjects, including mental health. The "How To Start Therapy" episode covers several common obstacles faced by those seeking therapy.

Openpathcollective.org is a US-based nationwide directory of affordable (between $30 and $60 per individual session) mental health providers.

REFERENCES

Conner, Tamlin S., Colin G. DeYoung, and Paul J. Silvia. November 17, 2016. "Everyday Creative Activity as a Path to Flourishing." *The Journal of Positive Psychology* 13 (2), 181–189. doi.org/10.1080/17439760.2016.1257049.

Hinchey, Liza M. 2018. "Mindfulness-Based Art Therapy: A Review of the Literature." *Inquiries* 10 (5). inquiriesjournal.com/articles/1737/mindfulness-based-art-therapy -a-review-of-the-literature.

Jalāl al-Dīn, Rūmī. 2004. *The Essential Rumi: New Expanded Edition*. Translated by Coleman Barks. San Francisco: HarperOne.

Juul, Lise, Karen Johanne Pallesen, Jaco Piet, Christine Parsons, and Lone Overby Fjorback. December 19, 2017. "Effectiveness of Mindfulness-Based Stress Reduction in a Self-Selecting and Self-Paying Community Setting." *Mindfulness* 9 (4), 1288–1298. doi.org/10.1007/s12671-017-0873-0.

Rappaport, Laury. 2014. *Mindfulness and the Arts Therapies: Theory and Practice*. Philadelphia: Jessica Kingsley Publishers.

Stuckey, Heather L. and Jeremy Nobel. February 2010. "The Connection Between Art, Healing, and Public Health: A Review of Current Literature." *American Journal of Public Health* 100 (2), 254–263. doi.org/10.2105/ajph.2008.156497.

Tang, Yi-Yuan, Britta K. Hölzel, and Michael I. Posner. March 18, 2015. "The Neuroscience of Mindfulness Meditation." *Nature Reviews Neuroscience* 16, 213–225. doi.org/10.1038/nrn3916.

Vago, David R. and Fadel Zeidan. July 11, 2016. "The Brain on Silent: Mind Wandering, Mindful Awareness, and States of Mental Tranquility." *Annals of the New York Academy of Sciences* 1373 (1), 96–113. doi.org/10.1111/nyas.13171.

Weir, Kirsten. April 1, 2022. "The Science Behind Creativity." *Monitor on Psychology* 53 (3), 40. Accessed August 4, 2022. apa.org/monitor/2022/04/cover-science-creativity.

INDEX

Acknowledgments

It was such a gift to write this book. Thanks to my editor, Alexis, for her kindness and expertise. Gratitude to my supportive friends, especially Ali, Nicole, and Nikoo. Special acknowledgment to my clients for their insights and wisdom. Finally, so much love to Chris, Emi, and Aya.

About the Author

Jennie Powe Runde, MFT, REAT, is an expressive arts therapist and facilitator working with people exploring identity at the intersection of race, sexuality, gender, class, spirituality, and dis/ability status. Her background and training include attachment theory, narrative therapy, and mindfulness-based approaches. Connect and learn more at expressiveartstherapist.com.